TELL ME WHY YOU FLED

TRUE STORIES OF SEEKING REFUGE

KAREN O'REILLY

Black Rose Writing | Texas

ISBN: 978-1-68433-391-2
PUBLISHED BY BLACK ROSE WRITING
www.blackrosewriting.com

Printed in the United States of America
Suggested Retail Price (SRP) $18.95

Tell Me Why You Fled is printed in Calluna

*As a planet-friendly publisher, Black Rose Writing does its best to eliminate unnecessary waste to reduce paper usage and energy costs, while never compromising the reading experience. As a result, the final word count vs. page count may not meet common expectations.

Praise for
Tell Me Why You Fled

"In this debut memoir, O'Reilly recounts her experiences working with refugees and accuses a humanitarian aid agency of corruption and hypocrisy. While visiting Zagreb, Croatia, in the year 2000, when she was in her 20s, the author met Agata, an Italian woman who was interning for the United Nations in Bosnia and Herzegovina. Agata had earned a master's degree in human rights — something that the author, who once aspired to be a human rights lawyer, didn't know was possible. O'Reilly moved to London in 2002 to pursue the same degree, and took a job in Uganda four years later, eager to trade her current life, which included the use of recreational drugs, for a 'different kind of living on the edge.' In Kampala, she found a diverse refugee community seeking assistance, and her job was to assess suitability for relocation—a task for which she readily admits she was unprepared: 'People's lives hinged on conclusions that we were unqualified to make.' She encountered people who were fleeing war and persecution in Sudan, Eritrea, Rwanda, and Somalia, among other locations. With unalloyed frankness, O'Reilly accuses the agency for which she worked of callousness, venality, and general incompetence. She says that she encountered casual racism, sexual harassment, and a culture of cowardice; one high-ranking commissioner, she says, was found to have been guilty of sexual harassment, and then given an award upon his resignation. The author also poignantly chronicles the heartbreaking plights of those she was charged with helping. Overall, O'Reilly writes simply but elegantly, without a hint of sentimentality but with plenty of emotion and provocative thought. And although her criticism of her profession is scathing, she impressively doesn't spare herself from scrutiny: 'I was beginning to wonder if we were quick to accuse refugees of lying because it let us off the hook. If refugees were lying anyway, what did it matter if our work was sloppy, if we were lazy, if we earned thousands of dollars per month while they lived in squalid camps and slums?'

A lucid critique of a humanitarian organization."
— *Kirkus Reviews*

"This is a poignant, heartbreakingly-honest book. Karen O'Reilly has sat behind the desk in muggy African offices where desperate refugees, their lives ripped apart by war, famine and ethnic hatred, interact with a lumbering, misogynistic UN bureaucracy theoretically dedicated to offering them new hope. Her beautifully-written account is unflinching, and

mercilessly self-critical concerning what it is to be a privileged expatriate working in the developing world, while brimming with compassion, empathy and insight."
— Michela Wrong, author of *Borderlines*

"In *Tell Me Why You Fled*, Karen O'Reilly puts a human face on some of the world's most vulnerable citizens. Imagine being the aid worker responsible for assembling the narrative that will – or won't – bring a safer future to a person who's never known safety. We're right there with her as she gently pulls their stories out, rooting for each of them. And at the end, we're right there with Karen again, questioning the multi-billion dollar humanitarian aid industry that leaves most behind."
— Heidi Postlewait, author of *Emergency Sex (and Other Desperate Measures): True Stories from a War Zone*

"Karen O'Reilly writes of her work resettling African refugees with striking empathy, and a sense of perspective that makes this book at once a compelling account of her experience, a critique of an inefficient resettlement system, and a brave and humane chronicle of the people involved. From the bureaucrats to the workers to the refugees, this is the story of people living between worlds, and, as she puts it, 'trying to piece together the puzzle of how to survive.' *Tell Me Why You Fled* is the best memoir I've read in a long, long time."
— Justin St. Germain, author of *Son of a Gun*

"An unflinchingly honest and important exploration of the hypocrisies of the aid industry, told with both sensitivity and a healthy dose of self-deprecation. The insider's view of the broken asylum system, where some of the world's most destitute people are stripped of their humanity and reduced to statistics and soundbites, it is a vital contribution to the debate, while also being enormously readable. *Tell Me Why You Fled* explores this important issue without ever losing sight of the human beings at the heart of it all."
— Charlotte McDonald Gibson, author of *Cast Away: True Stories of Survival from Europe's Refugee Crisis*

"*Tell Me Why You Fled* is a riveting work of witness, unflinching and deeply sympathetic in its true stories of people for whom so much more than home has been taken, ravaged, destroyed. With bracing candor, Karen O'Reilly illuminates the often absurd world of humanitarian aid and resettlement in which she asks herself, Why do I do this work? Who can hold such terrible stories? Who am I trying to save? How can I do good, remain sane, when so much seems hopeless, forever wrong, when there is no escaping my own complicity?"
— Gregory Martin, author of *Stories for Boys*

"There's a huge, global organization — the United Nations High Commissioner for Refugees — whose job is to look after millions of people who've lost their homes to war and oppression. Peel back the titles and money and false gravitas and you'll find corrupt profiteers, sexual predators, religious bigots. But listen to me. Scatter the cynics and what remains are people who, believe it or not, really, truly want to help. Their reasons are messy. Their own needs don't always make for acceptable conversation at dinner parties. But they're good people, and desperately sympathetic. UNHCR is just the uniform they wear. UNHCR-veteran Karen O'Reilly's lovely little book is about these good people. It's funny. It's gross. And beneath its gentle prose about young mothers and Ugandan gin, it's white-hot angry. Angry at the evil men who start the wars. At the supposed pious who reject people for their skin, their nationality, their sexuality, at the bosses who groped her. At her fellow first-worlders who just don't understand. At herself for failing, time and again, to save everyone. About two-thirds of the way through, I couldn't see through my own tears. 'I didn't want to die while there were still books, or places or people out there that I loved, or could still love,' Karen wrote. I know good people, millions of them, share this sentiment. Thank God."
— David Axe, author of *War is Boring*

"Honest, haunting and hilarious, *Tell me Why You Fled* beautifully and unblinkingly lays out the extremes of the humanitarian aid industry. Through O'Reilly we peer into the intertwining lives of refugees and the people working to assist them. A touching story of human connection and self-insight."
— Jessica Alexander, author of *Chasing Chaos: My Decade In and Out of Humanitarian Aid*

"There are books, and there are bracing acts of whistleblowing. *Tell Me Why You Fled* suckers you in as the personal story of a young Irish woman who sets out for a new life in equatorial Africa, unfolds as travelogue, and gradually reveals itself as something different. O'Reilly tells the dirty secrets the United Nations don't put in their ads. Poverty is a nice little earner. This is a book that took real guts. Ironic, given that the author's running theme is her own depression at feeling useless. If just one of the monsters in this book faces questions as a result of these pages, she can rest easy she has been less extremely useful indeed."
— Jane Bussman, author of *The Worst Date Ever: or How it Took a Comedy Writer to Expose Joseph Kony and Africa's Secret War*

"A book about vulnerable people in ravaged places and the efforts to provide help. Karen is wise to the nuances of aid work and honest about the personal distress that can run alongside it. An important read about refugees and human frailty."
— Stuart Bailie, BBC broadcaster and author of *Trouble Songs*

Semifinalist, Kore Press Memoir Award, judged by *Cheryl Strayed*

For Judah, Noah, and Albie: my home

Tell Me Why You Fled

True Stories of Seeking Refuge

Contents

I. What It's Like

What It's Like

I was sleeping when the office called to say Sadia had doused herself in gasoline and was trying to set herself alight.

It was 2007, and I was working for the United Nations High Commissioner for Refugees – UNHCR – in Kampala. My role was to interview the most vulnerable refugees who had fled to Uganda from various parts of east and central Africa, and persuade wealthy countries to give them a permanent home. Somali refugees I worked with were resettled to some of the coldest parts of the US, Congolese families found homes in Australia, a whole Sudanese community was relocated to a tiny village in the west of Ireland. Some refugees sent updates, emails from their new countries – *Thank you for sending me here! I love Canada, chicken and chips, and Red Bull!* Most, I never heard from again.

Sadia was a sixteen-year-old Somali refugee, one of the first clients I'd been assigned when I'd arrived the year before. I knew her story from interviews I'd conducted with her, and from her file, which predated me. According to the naming convention used in Somalia, she should have had three names: her first name, followed by her father's name, then her grandfather's. But Sadia had been abandoned as a baby, and no one knew who her father or grandfather was, so "Sadia" was the only name she had. A couple with no children of their own had found her on the street in Mogadishu, and taken her in and raised her. The couple's family, neighbors, and friends shunned the child, calling her a "bastard" and an "outcast." Since Sadia's biological father was unknown, so, critically, was her clan. This created the possibility, neighbors said, that she was a Midgan – a member of one of the lowliest tribes in Somalia – and so she was treated, as all Midgans were, with contempt.

I put down the phone, looked around, tugged the ends of the mosquito net out from beneath the mattress, and climbed out of bed. I pulled on clothes from the floor, not checking if they were clean, and called Paul, the boda-boda – motorbike taxi – driver I always used, asking him to come as soon as he could. A breeze blew through the open, but barred, bedroom windows, causing the strings that hung from the freed mosquito net to flutter gently. Outside, it was cool, cloudy: the rainy season had just begun.

The office was a five-minute ride, downhill, from where I lived. I used one hand, always, to hold the back of the boda driver's seat, the other to try to balance the mug of coffee I never had time to drink at home. Paul was used to this eccentricity of mine – the boda-back cup of coffee – and took the turns slowly.

The smell of gasoline hit me as soon as we reached the office car park. The guards at the gate told me Sadia was in the cafeteria bathroom, changing out of her gasoline-soaked dress. They had seized the matches from her as she'd tried to light one. My colleague had found her some clothes: a T-shirt and stretch pants, though Sadia always wore a Somali dress and veil. A driver had gone to another colleague's house to fetch her an African dress.

I waited in the cafeteria for Sadia to change and ordered toast and more coffee. The cafeteria lady brought the toast, white and smeared with margarine, with a Thermos of local coffee and a chipped cup. She sat them before me, unsmiling.

The cafeteria was in a veranda, under a corrugated iron roof supported by pillars on three sides. Sadia came out from the bathroom wearing the baggy T-shirt and purple stretch pants. She was unveiled and had, I saw for the first time, chin-length ringletted hair. The cafeteria lady, gathering dishes from a corner table now, looked her over with an expression of contempt. I returned her expression, and she scowled and looked away. I could guess at the source of her disdain: Sadia was dirty and scrappy, and Muslim, while the cafeteria lady was immaculately-dressed and Christian. Sadia's suicide attempt would be seen, most likely, as nothing more than attention-seeking, a way to gain entry to the office, where refugees weren't normally received, and secure an audience with resettlement staff. On another occasion, a senior manager told us that a refugee who had attempted suicide by throwing himself in front of a car was just "having a tantrum." He sent an email out to say that we should not respond to such behavior, or encourage it; that refugees who behaved like this were merely trying to manipulate us into being resettled to the West. My colleagues, upon receiving the email, mumbled in agreement. "Suicide attempts," another staff member noted, "are just a way to jump the queue."

"Your hair is lovely," I told Sadia. Without the veil, she seemed even younger. When I'd met her before, she had appeared feisty and stubborn. Now she looked vulnerable, scared. I reached my hand out to comfort her, then let it drop. This wasn't my role, I had been reminded over and over: I was to stay removed, assess her case impartially, unemotionally, put her forward for resettlement only if I was certain everything she said was true. She sat down. She was tiny. Her legs were shaking. I stared at her. She was barely more than a child.

Sadia's adoptive parents, I knew, had died when she was twelve, and after that, she had lived alone. With no one protecting her, men broke into her house and raped her. She had become pregnant from the rape and was thirteen when her daughter was born. The baby's only name was Fawzia, since her father and grandfather, like Sadia's, were unknown. When Fawzia was three months old, another group of men abducted Sadia from her house, leaving her daughter behind. Sadia never saw Fawzia again. The men took Sadia with them in a car but later threw her out when she drove them crazy with her crying. She walked to the nearest village and hitched rides to Kenya, then Uganda. In Uganda, other Somalis shunned her, calling her a "bastard" and – worse – a *Christian*. For two years, Sadia lived in a makeshift hut in a refugee settlement on her own. Finally, she sold all her possessions – her plastic bucket, her pot, her bowl – and used the money to come to Kampala, where she lived in a hut in a slum on the edge of town.

I leaned towards Sadia. "Will you eat?"

"I don't eat these days," she said shrugging. "I have no appetite."

I gazed at her. "You're too thin."

She bit her lower lip and looked to the ground.

"Will you have half of my bread and some tea?"

She nodded reluctantly, and I passed my plate to her. She picked at the surface of the toast, biting from the top and not into it. The cafeteria lady brought her black tea, and she drank half a cup. I took out a cigarette but left it on the table. The air was still thick with gasoline fumes.

I turned to Sadia and said, "Talk to me."

She looked away and began to cry. "Life is too difficult. I'm tired of trying." She pushed the bread away and tried to wipe her tears. They were falling onto the T-shirt.

I didn't say anything. I wanted to at least take her hand, to hold it in mine. Colleagues walked past the cafeteria, staring as they caught sight of us. The cafeteria lady tried to take Sadia's bread. I told her, too harshly, "Please leave it be."

A colleague arrived with the African dress. It was nylon and brown, with an elaborate lace collar, and it was an even worse fit than the T-shirt and stretch pants. Sadia pulled it on over the other clothes. The neck fell down over each shoulder. She tried to hitch it up. She looked like a child in a school play. She pressed the heels of her hands to her eyes.

"Life is too much suffering," she said.

The smell of gasoline was nauseating. I pulled her hands gently from her eyes. Her wrists were bird-thin.

"Please, Sadia, will you eat."

She looked at me, bit the toast, and pushed it away.

"It doesn't mean things won't change," I said. "It's still possible that when you're, say, thirty, things will be very different."

She stared at me. "When I was thirteen, they weren't different, they were the same."

"No," I said, "not thirteen, thirty – old, like me." I gestured at myself to make the point, trying to appear more convinced than I was.

Sadia looked at me with raised eyebrows and lifted the cup, then sat it down. It was beginning to rain – a sudden, heavy tropical rain that rattled the roof of the cafeteria.

"What do you want to do when you're older?" I asked her.

She spoke quietly. "I want to work with refugees because I know what their lives are like."

I nodded and looked away. I had learned that many of my colleagues didn't know, and didn't want to know what refugees' lives were like. Eventually, I came to wonder if I really wanted to know either. It was easier not to know, not to believe it: then I could ignore the consequences of the fact that we were giving the most vulnerable refugees forty dollars a month to live on, while a senior staff member had told me that he earned, with allowances, two hundred thousand dollars a year. Even my monthly stipend as a "volunteer" was over forty times the amount that the neediest refugees received.

I turned to Sadia. "What will you do if you're accepted by another country?"

She slid her hands under her knees and sat up. "I want to go to school. I've never been. My adoptive parents taught me to read and write at home."

I nodded. "Did they teach you English?"

Sadia looked bemused. "They didn't know English. They only knew Somali and Italian."

I smiled. On occasion, I forgot about Italy's colonial rule in Somalia. Once, early on, Sadia had told me that she missed Somali food. I asked her, curious, what a typical Somali dish was. "Pasta!" she said, as though it was obvious. "Spaghetti!"

"So how did you learn English?" I asked her.

She shrugged. "I learned it from newspapers that people left in the trash."

"In the trash where?"

"In the camp. People would throw out old papers and leaflets and things. I would pick them out of the trash, bring them home and read them to try to make sense of the articles, using the pictures. That helped me learn a lot of different words."

I looked at her. I pictured her carefully picking out the discarded papers, shaking out the rubbish that stuck between their pages, bringing them to the hut that she lived in alone, poring over them, sifting through to try to understand words in their context, memorizing them, trying them out. Her English was almost fluent.

"If you're resettled," I said, "you'll be placed with a foster family. You're OK with that?"

Sadia shrugged. "For three years, I've been living on my own. I don't need a family."

"I don't think you have a choice," I told her, "until you're eighteen. They'll place you with a foster family until then."

She looked away. "I know how to take care of myself."

She smoothed her dress over her knees. Her eyes had teared up again. She brought her hands to them, discreetly, turned her head away and rubbed them as though something, dust perhaps, had gotten into them.

"Maybe," I said quietly, "there'll be a time in your life when things are so good that you won't remember how this felt."

Sadia played with the folds of her dress between her knees. "I'm too tired."

I looked outside. The rain was turning the red earth to mud. The office was surrounded by tropical gardens inside a walled compound. We had been told that refugees must not be allowed to make scenes at the gate to the compound, because this was a nice neighborhood – full of embassies and ambassadors' residences. A rule had been instituted that refugees could no longer come to see staff at the office at all, but would have to meet us at the run-down premises of a local refugee organization on the other side of town.

The cafeteria lady returned. I let her take the half-eaten bread. The rain was easing. "Sadia," I said, "would you like to see our office?"

She turned away, wiped her eyes with her sleeves, and shrugged. We stood up, and she tripped on the hem of the dress. I put my arm around her, gathering the dress up between her shoulders so it wouldn't trail in the mud. We stepped outside. The rain had cleansed the air. It was warm, fresh. The office building was painted white, and the windows, like the windows on my house, were barred. We mounted the steps. My colleagues stared up from their desks. I shouldn't have my arm around Sadia. I shouldn't have brought her inside.

We entered my office. My desk was stacked high with other refugees' files. I looked at Sadia. She would most likely be resettled to the US. I tried to picture her in a high school there, surrounded by other sixteen-year-olds, bored, playing with their phones, complaining about homework, chatting about clothes and parties. How would she explain her life to other teenagers there? Would she feel even worse? Could anything make up for what she had been through? I thought too about myself at her age, self-harming as well, attempting suicide as a cry for help, though my life was a world away from hers.

Resettlement in itself, I knew, wasn't going to give Sadia what she needed. Often, when refugees were interviewed by staff in the countries to which they'd been resettled, they said they felt lonely and isolated. It was a price they sometimes wondered whether they should have paid for an increase in material comfort and safety. Pride often stopped them from saying these things to the families they had left behind. People who couldn't find work in the US still found ways to send money to their families in refugee camps. The reality of resettlement – living in poverty and isolation in a country with a different culture, a different language – wasn't transmitted to those left behind, and so an idealized picture of a new life overseas was maintained. I did the same thing, I realized: I didn't tell family or friends at home what my work was actually like – that I wasn't always helping people, that refugees weren't even allowed to enter our offices, that staff, even "volunteers" like me, took home handsome allowances while refugees lived in squalor. I didn't say that we had maids whom we paid pitifully. This wasn't what people where I came from – Ireland, the West – wanted to hear.

There were no trained counselors in our office, but there was one, a woman called Miriam, working at the office of the organization where we interviewed clients. I didn't even know if she was available – she sometimes had a waiting list. But I could bring Sadia to her, introduce her, ensure she had an appointment or at least a place on the list. I could ask for Sadia's resettlement case to be expedited, but it would still be months before she would be accepted – if a country did accept her – and weeks, months, even years after that before she would leave. She would need help until then.

I turned to Sadia. "Can I bring you to a counselor?"

She nodded vaguely. I wasn't sure she'd heard me, or understood. I was even less sure the counselor would be helpful. I didn't know how to help Sadia, at least not while she was my client. If she weren't my client, it was my naive fantasy, I could bring her to my home, protect her, make her feel safe. I wondered though, whether in this fantasy, it was her – or myself at her age – that I was trying to help. I wondered, always, whether I was trying to *rescue* my younger self – by doing this work, by helping refugees find a safer home.

I reached for the phone and called a driver to bring us to the office where the counselor was based. Sadia sat at the empty desk across from mine while I gathered files for other refugees I was meeting that day. She stared out the window. After a while, the driver called to say we could leave. I stuffed the files into a case with a laptop to type notes from interviews, and heaved the strap up over my shoulder. I said to Sadia, "The driver's ready."

She didn't stand. She pushed up the sleeves of the nylon dress – they were falling over her hands. She said, "You have no idea what it's like."

I gazed at her. I wished we'd been able to find something that fitted her. I reached out my hand to pull the sleeve up from her shoulder again, then let it drop.

I reached out again and touched her hair this time, tucked a stray ringlet behind her ear, let my hand graze her cheek. I said, "I know."

II. Defined by War

Defined by War

My room in a slum building in Prague came with no bathroom, only access to a rat-infested shared toilet whose smell made me retch. I slept on a slab of yellow sponge in the middle of the floor. I cooked all my meals in a toasted-sandwich maker, the only appliance I owned.

It was 1999, and I was twenty-four. Like my expatriate friends, I had come to Prague while backpacking around Eastern Europe and had planned to stay a few days or a week, but never left. We'd been sucked in by cheap Pilsner and underground parties, and found work as unqualified English teachers to pay for the Absinthe and beer. We lived in the grungiest neighborhoods in the city – the few neighborhoods that hadn't changed since the dissolution of Czechoslovakia in 1993. On the evenings I didn't go out, I'd bring an empty two-liter plastic Fanta bottle to a bar, and a phlegmatic bartender would fill it with Budvar or Krušovice for me to take home. I tried drugs, not sure, sometimes, what they were. I would drink all night, and fall asleep on the tram home, waking only when the driver told me that we'd reached the end of the line. I'd get off, wait for another tram in the opposite direction, and then fall asleep on that one too, and be driven past my stop once again.

As well as accidental expats, many of my friends were refugees and immigrants from the former Yugoslavia. I dated a Serbian man who'd feigned illness to escape service in the army during the war. My closest friend was a Croatian refugee whose town had been held under siege for months and almost entirely destroyed. Several times a week, I ate ćevapi – lumpy, grilled sausages – with flatbread, raw onions, and a spicy red sauce, at a restaurant belonging to a couple who'd fled Bosnia some years before. I drank šljivovica – home-made plum brandy – with their children, who were teenagers when they fled.

I had been a teenager too, when the Yugoslav war had unfolded. I had watched reports of killings and cities under siege on the portable television in the kitchen of our house in Northern Ireland. The war seemed so remote, though it wasn't geographically far away, and Northern Ireland was enduring its own conflict. That conflict – *The Troubles* – had begun before I was born and I hadn't known anything else, but I didn't think about it. It was like the rain, the gloomy weather: always there, in the background. My friends and I, when asked about it by American tourists or Spanish exchange students, would shrug. We grew up hearing bombs in the distance, evacuating our schools because of bomb scares, and seeing the handwritten signs taped to shop windows: *Bomb damage sale. 20% off!* But as teenagers, we didn't want to talk about it. We wanted to talk about American indie bands, and Salinger and Vonnegut, and the French Impressionist paintings that featured in the calendars on our bedroom walls. The Northern Irish conflict was provincial. We refused to be defined by it.

The Yugoslav war took place elsewhere, on TV. Those affected by it had nothing in common with us. They wore unfashionable clothes, we assumed, and listened to dated music. Unlike us, they *were* defined by war.

But the teenagers who had fled Bosnia and Croatia as refugees, I saw belatedly in Prague, had listened to the same alternative music we had. They had snuck off to drink vodka in parks after dark, as we had, and formed punk bands. They read and wrote poetry. They dressed in black. They weren't *other* to us, any more than we were *other* to the American students I had met in Dublin, who didn't believe we listened to the same bands they did, and who asked, surprised, *you have gay people in Ireland?*

What had been confined to TV news reports – *war in Yugoslavia* – was made real. Refugees weren't simply indistinguishable columns of people moving through fields in headscarves and shawls. They were Pavement fans with nose rings, who wrote poetry. They were like the friends I had grown up with. They were like me.

I wanted to see the countries my friends had lived in and fled from, and in the summer of 2000, when I was twenty-five, I set off to travel around the former Yugoslavia alone.

I rode a bus from Prague to Zagreb, then buses and trains along the Croatian coast. I took ferries to islands where old men tried to seduce me, and drank Karlovačko beer alone in street-side cafes. I stayed in the apartments of elderly women who approached me at train stations and ferry terminals, to say they were renting their spare rooms for the equivalent of five dollars a night. I read books about the war, and talked to strangers. I befriended twentysomething locals – men and women – and was invited to their apartments too.

At a hostel in Zagreb, I met an Italian woman, Agata, who was my age. She told me she was interning for UNHCR – the United Nations High Commissioner for Refugees – in Livno in Bosnia, and invited me to stay with her. The only thing I knew about UNHCR was that they had helped my friends who owned the Bosnian restaurant when they had fled for Prague.

Agata was staying in a guesthouse in Livno, in a room with two narrow single beds. I spent three nights with her and visited the UNHCR office. There were maps on the wall, and whiteboards noting in blue and red marker the percentages of the different ethnic groups – Croat, Bosniak, Serb – in various regions of Bosnia. The office was working on repatriation of refugees who had formerly fled the area around Livno, and who had now chosen to return. In some instances, the refugees' homes had been taken over illegally in their absence, and UNHCR staff were monitoring evictions. In case of problems between those returning and those being evicted, members of the UN International Police Task Force – IPTF – stepped in. Agata discussed the details of an upcoming eviction that she was attending with a colleague.

I was fascinated. I felt envious – and small. My job in Prague involved chatting with employees of Czech Telecom – in my native language. They wanted to practice their English conversation skills, and my only task was to facilitate this. Classes began at 7am, and I arrived on occasion still drunk from the night before. I had a three-hour lunch break, and I would use this to take the Metro home and sleep off my hangover, before returning to chat again – about my students' plans for the weekend, Ireland, their jobs.

At university in Dublin, I had studied law for one year, with the dream of becoming a human rights lawyer. Instead, I learned how a man who tripped on the road was able to claim a huge sum of money from the Government, and a woman who asked a train conductor to wake her up at the location of her job interview tried to sue him when he didn't. I was depressed by students who lined up outside the law library before it opened to hide journals from that week's lecture so that no one else could read them. I abandoned the course to study English Literature in Edinburgh.

I graduated not knowing what I wanted to do. After graduation, I filed claims in order of policy number in the basement of an insurance firm we called the Graduate Graveyard. The policy numbers were eight digits long, and I would see them when I closed my eyes at night. To ease the boredom, I listened to *Remembrance of Things Past* on my Walkman. The audiobook took up more than thirty cassettes.

I entered data and manned a phone line for queries about mortgages that I understood nothing about. I gave terrible financial advice. When a man wrote to the mortgage company I worked for, expressing his contempt that we addressed him in our letters as "Mr" instead of "Lord," I went into our database and changed his prefix to "Time Lord." Now all his mortgage statements would address him as though he were Dr Who.

I moved to San Francisco for three months and operated the lights at a gay and lesbian theatre. I stayed, rent-free, in a hostel in North Beach in return for making breakfast, and was fired for putting too much peanut butter on bagels. From there, I moved to Prague, where I asked Czech Telecom workers about their weekends, forgetting, often, to listen to their answers.

Agata was helping people who had fled war return to their homes.

Agata told me that she was not a lawyer, but had studied Arts, and then completed an MA in Human Rights, for which you didn't need a legal background. I had no idea this kind of degree was a possibility.

At an Irish bar in Livno, I met Agata's friends, who were all officers with the IPTF. One, an English man called Philip, was visiting Livno from Sarajevo, and he offered to bring me to Sarajevo when he returned there the next day.

Philip picked me up in his car, a white Landcruiser with a black "UN" emblazoned on the hood and sides, and a huge antenna for receiving radio signals. An official peacekeeper's vehicle. People watched as we got in. I felt exotic, important.

Philip took me on a tour of Sarajevo. Many of the buildings were still riddled with bullet holes. We drove past a building that had belonged to a newspaper called *Oslobodenje. Liberation.* Only the shell of it remained. I asked Philip why it had not yet been rebuilt. "They want people to be reminded of what happened," he told me. "They want visitors to the city to bear witness."

We drove to the Sarajevo Tunnel Museum, marked by a small, hand-printed sign on the side of the road. The tunnel, Philip told me, had been built by the Bosnian army during the siege of Sarajevo. It ran under the Sarajevo airport runway. It linked Sarajevo, which was cut off by Serbian forces, to Bosnian-held territory on the other side of the airport. The tunnel enabled humanitarian aid, food, and weapons to reach Sarajevo, and allowed people to get out. The tunnel's builders were paid with cigarettes.

Now a museum had been built onto the house whose cellar had served as the entrance to the tunnel. The owner of the house ran the museum, showed visitors around, and explained its role to them.

We knocked on the door, and a small, stooped man answered. Philip asked him if we could come in to look, and he fetched his son, who spoke English. His son brought us through to the entrance of the tunnel. Philip, having been before, stood waiting outside. I walked alone through part of it, touching the ceiling and sides with my fingers. It was small and cold. I tried to imagine people there, fleeing the shelling in the city. I came back outside. Philip was standing with his hands in his pockets. "Everything alright?"

I nodded.

He reached out and touched my arm. "We'll get something to eat soon."

We went back into the house, and the man's son indicated that we should sit. We waited as he inserted a video cassette into the VCR on the dresser in front of us. The picture shook and then came into view. The video showed how the tunnel was used, and some of the devastation that was taking place outside it. I bit my thumbnail as I watched. There were souvenirs for sale around the room, copies of the video on the table beside us, and flags tacked to the walls. When the video ended, Philip stood and placed some money in the boy's hand. I looked at the photos on the walls, and read the descriptions, typed and Scotch-taped beneath them. I thanked the boy and followed Philip out to the car.

After leaving the museum, we drove to a hill outside Sarajevo. "You shouldn't go hiking elsewhere, because of mines," Philip said as we got out of the car. "But this area has been cleared. Take my hand."

We watched our steps carefully. We reached the top of the hill, and the city opened up below us: houses, hospitals, museums, mosques, cemeteries. "This is what the snipers would have seen when they were shooting from here," Philip said. He pointed out an Olympic arena, built for the Winter Games. "During the war," he told me, "the arena became a cemetery for those killed in conflict."

Earlier, we had visited one of the war cemeteries. The dead had been born around the time that I was.

1974-1992
1972-1994
1975-1993

I could make out the tombstones jutting out from the middle of the arena. I imagined the people, young men, mostly, who had been killed. Men who, if they had survived, might have been like my friend Vedran, who played bass in a punk band. Or Marko, who played pool with, always, a cigarette clamped between his lips. Or Vlad, who taught me all his chess tricks over beers, but whom I could never beat.

They were gone.

We made our way back along the ragged path on the hill. Philip took my hand again as I struggled, in flip-flops, to make my way down. When we reached the road, he didn't let go until we came to the car.

In the evening, we walked along the streets of the Old Town. The city was beautiful. The dark green scrubby hills formed a backdrop to the terracotta rooftops and the pale green dome of the mosque. Pigeons flew amongst the old stone walls and pecked their way through the cobbled streets. They flocked at the feet of an old man who kept peach-colored plastic cups full of corn kernels, with which to feed them.

Suddenly, as I watched, a boy ran a figure eight in ribbons through the pigeons, firing a plastic gun. The birds circled and swooped, terrified, shrieking and batting their wings.

Throughout the city, I noticed red splotches in the sidewalk and asked Philip what they were. "Sarajevo Roses," he told me. "The concrete was pockmarked by mortar shells, and the scars were later filled with red resin. To ensure we don't forget."

They looked like painted flowers. Like Rorschach tests. Like splattered blood.

So we don't forget.

In the narrow single bed in Philip's spare room that night, I dreamt that I was walking on the roses and had become confused, thinking they were mines. I was crying, unable to avoid them. Philip hugged me, reassuring me that the mines were no longer there. I woke, disoriented, unable to figure out where I was. I wanted to call Philip and to ask him to hold me. I felt confused: I wasn't attracted to him - he was around twenty years older than I was, and, I suspected, much more conservative. But I suddenly felt afraid, and in his role and his kindness, and my confusion, he made me feel safe.

***

In Prague, we continued to drink, and to party, to take risks, and feel immune to anything bad happening to us. Then two Russian friends were arrested and imprisoned for overstaying their visas. An American friend was locked up for selling drugs. An Israeli friend, Dov, left Prague, and then we learned that he had died by suicide. He had jumped from a tall building. Many people came and left Prague, and I didn't see them again. I tried to tell myself that this was what had happened to Dov too. He had simply left. There was no reason for me to have to acknowledge that he was dead.

Then another friend, Steve, died. He had taken heroin and called a sex worker to come to his flat. He died while he was with her – he had accidentally overdosed – and she was forced to call the police. We had thought he was a good friend but realized when he died how little we knew about him. He was British. He had grey hair, which he wore in a ponytail. He played guitar. He had told me I had *the best ass in Prague*, and I had laughed it off. I asked his friend if it was true. He shrugged. "*One* of the best asses. I wouldn't say *the* best." Steve had argued with him, indignant. This absurd conversation was, I realized, the most vivid memory I had of him.

We didn't know how to contact Steve's family – we didn't know who they were, or where they lived. After they were finally tracked down and came to Prague to collect his body, we heard nothing. We didn't know if they had a memorial service, or where.

I read book after book on the former Yugoslavia and the war there. The ethnic cleansing. The genocide. I placed the photos I'd taken of the bombed-out buildings in a small plastic album that I'd bought in the shop that developed the photos. I felt strange about them and showed them to no one. Since my friends died, everything had felt suddenly urgent. I thought of Agata and the refugees she was helping to come home. I wanted to do something other than stay up all night drinking, with my life. I wanted to feel worthwhile.

I walked to an internet café in the evenings after work and began researching master's degrees in Human Rights.

I wasn't motivated only by a desire to feel useful, but by what I perceived to be the exoticism and glamour of the work. I wanted to travel on dirt roads, avoiding mines, in a mud-splattered Landcruiser. I wanted the special blue passport – the *Laissez Passer* – I knew UN staff had. I wanted to *feel* something, as I had wanted to feel something when I had self-harmed at fifteen, and taken risks in Prague at twenty-four. I wanted to switch from one kind of edgy life: drinking all night, sleeping in a slum, hanging out with drug dealers and drug addicts, for a different kind of living on the edge.

***

In 2002, the year I turned twenty-seven, I began an MA in Human Rights in London. There were just under fifty students and twenty-five nationalities in the class. There was a Czech journalist who had done undercover reporting on the treatment of Roma people, a Palestinian man who had headed up a human rights NGO in Gaza, and whose brother had been killed by the Israeli army, a Zambian teacher whose sister had just died from AIDS, and lawyers, activists and reporters from Indonesia and Egypt and Brazil. It was common, it would slowly emerge, to study human rights because of the injustices you had experienced in your own life. Trying to right a childhood of abuse – an alcoholic parent, a violent parent, sexual abuse – by fighting injustices outside of yourself, which somehow felt easier to do. If abusive childhoods could not be undone, perhaps it was possible to make up for them, by finding safe homes for other children. Children fleeing war. Refugees.

We dedicated ourselves to studying human rights and humanitarian law and interning at NGOs and, in 2003, to protesting the war in Iraq. We were earnest and enthusiastic and optimistic. Our professor told us: "Promise me one thing. Promise me that after years of doing this work, you won't become jaded. So many people in the human rights field start out enthusiastic and determined but eventually become disillusioned and cynical. Promise me that won't be you."

I would recall his words occasionally over the next years when I worked, first, in human rights education, and later with refugees.

Flower Paintings

In April of 2005, I had just turned thirty. I was living alone in a huge, squalid house in Dún Laoghaire, on the east coast of Ireland, a few miles from Dublin. The house was due to be gutted, but the landlord was renting it out to me in the meantime, more as a means of preventing squatters from moving in than of making money. Only one room of the house, a downstairs living room, was even vaguely habitable; it had a sofa, an old bed, and a Superser gas heater. The other rooms, which I only ventured into occasionally, still bore traces of the house's previous grubby tenancy: pages from soft porn magazines, broken polystyrene shells that had once contained burgers, old Coke cans. The furniture hadn't been replaced since the seventies, or perhaps earlier. The whole house smelled of rot.

Even in spring, the house was freezing. There were no appliances in the kitchen. I lived on take-out with the money I saved on rent.

I was working for Amnesty International, and the salary, like most NGO salaries, was low, but I was working three days a week, so earned only three-fifths of even that. When the organization secured a grant to employ me full-time, I began looking for new places to live.

One morning, I saw an advertisement for a room to let while browsing online during my lunch break. There were scanned photos of the rooms in the house. The kitchen had green leather armchairs with brass claw feet and a red tiled floor. There was a large, yellowing silver tray on the fireplace. Above the mantlepiece in the living room was a framed poster for an exhibition at the Botanic Gardens that I had seen only months before. At the top of the poster was written *Flower Paintings*, the title of the exhibition. Beneath the title were miniature watercolor illustrations of flowers, and their names in Latin. I had liked the exhibition. That the owner of this house had seen it and presumably liked like it too, felt like a sign. I scribbled the number on a napkin and went outside to call it.

The person on the other end of the phone told me that her name was Martha. She said that the house belonged to her, and her roommate had just moved out to live with her boyfriend. She was a journalist who wrote about environmental issues. I told her I worked in human rights education. She said to come by the next day.

I could smell fried onions as I waited at the front door the following evening. Martha answered, holding a wooden spoon, stuck with onion slices. She ushered me down narrow stairs to the kitchen. The house was one room wide and staggered over five levels. A pot was simmering on a gas stove. A black cat sat in anticipation on the wooden table. Another, almost identical, was curled, sleeping, on the green chair beside the fireplace. Martha stirred the pot and wiped her hands on a cloth napkin by the stove. She pointed to the cats, smiling. "This one's Topsy, and the sleeping one's Turvy."

She filled a kettle and placed it on the ring beside the pot. I sat by the table and reached to stroke the cat. It miaowed and jumped to the floor, stretched, walked to Martha, and rubbed itself back and forth, purring, against her ankles.

She put a tablespoon in the pot, blew on it and tasted it.

"What are you making?" I asked her.

"French onion soup." She gestured to the pot. "Would you like to stay and eat?"

I shook my head. "Thank you, but no. Just the tea is good."

Martha nodded and lifted the kettle, which was beginning to shriek. "Human rights education work sounds amazing. And really good. I mean, a good thing to do." She paused. "My work is mostly meaningless."

I looked around. The wall behind the table was sloped, where it ran under the stairs. There was a white painted bookcase, stacked high with old cookery books, folders, scrapbooks with recipe cuttings sticking out, old Vogue magazines. The windowsill beside the stove was cluttered with herb plants.

"But your work is worthwhile. You write about environmental issues?"

Martha nodded vaguely. "I have one column about sustainable living. But mostly – I used to write a dating column. I still write about things like that. Dating, lifestyle, I don't know – make-up. All fluff." She poured the boiling water into an orange tin teapot. "But what you do sounds so useful."

I shook my head. "I guess. I mean, I like it. We do a lot of art stuff – help fifteen and sixteen-year-olds make plays and films about human rights issues. But," I paused. "I don't know if it's always meaningful. Or as meaningful as you'd think."

I knew as I spoke how the job sounded to others: writing books on human rights, encouraging schools to teach them, bringing education on racism, gay rights, and refugee rights to thousands of teenagers. I knew that it sounded *good.* I knew, in the abstract, that I should have been satisfied, even proud. But I couldn't feel it. I had a boyfriend, Michael, who was kind and affectionate, but uninterested in taking our relationship further – in moving in together, or even seeing each other more than occasionally. His lack of commitment reinforced my belief that I was inadequate.

I had problems sleeping and was exhausted and distracted at work. I had become obsessed with my insomnia, convinced that if I could only sleep, I would feel fine. I bought over-the-counter sleeping pills, herbal pills, teas, balms to rub on my temples. I had thyroid tests and wore a complicated device with wires stuck to my chest for a night to determine if I had a heart problem. All the tests came back negative. I ordered a contraption that, if I held a button during the hours that I was awake at night, would tell me exactly how much sleep I was actually getting. I bought self-help books, workbooks, books with ridiculous titles: *Desperately Seeking Snoozin'.* Two weeks before, my doctor had proposed gently, "You know that your insomnia is a symptom of your depression and not the cause?" He reached for a box of Kleenex when I cried. He came around the desk to give me the Kleenex and placed his hand on my arm. His kindness had made me cry more.

Martha lifted two tall mugs from a shelf and sat across from me. "I go to some of Amnesty's fundraisers – I was at the concert last month." She poured the tea, then stood up suddenly. The cat that had climbed onto her lap jumped quickly down. She stirred the soup again, tasted it, and turned the gas ring off. "Would you like to see the house?"

"Sure." I stood, still cradling the mug of tea.

Martha wiped her hands on the seat of her jeans. She was wearing an oversized shirt, beads, calf-length jeans, and flip-flops. She rubbed the belly of the cat who was waking, uncurling on the chair, and led me up the flights of stairs. We passed her bedroom, then a roof garden with folding pink metal chairs and table and different-sized potted plants.

The roof of the top bedroom slanted to the front wall. The floorboards and fireplace were painted white, the skirting boards a robin's egg blue. There were candles in the fireplace, huddled together in the grate. The legs of the desk were delicate, sculpted carefully at the feet.

"You have such lovely furniture," I said.

Martha laughed. "This desk, and the table downstairs – and the green leather chairs: I found them in a skip."

I raised my eyebrows. "Really? Someone threw these away?"

Martha nodded, smiling. "Just after I moved in. The sofa was tattered and falling apart, but I covered it with fabric I found in a charity shop."

We walked out onto the landing. Dresses and hats and bags hung from nails on the wall. Costume dresses – burgundy and dark green silk, with feather boas draped around the neck; flamboyant hats and bags with elaborate clasps. There was a stack of books on the floor in the corner.

I wanted this house to be my home.

The morning after I saw her house, Martha called me and left a message asking if I was still interested in the room. I hired two taxis to carry my cardboard boxes of books and a case of clothes and moved the following week.

By July 2005, I was no longer able to work. I was leaving the office for an hour once a week to attend group therapy. People in the group talked about their hypochondria: about their constant fear that they were ill and going to die. I didn't understand: I *wanted* to die. My regret was that I could not: I felt too bad about the effect on my family, on friends. I signed up for individual therapy, not realizing the therapist was a psychoanalyst. He didn't respond to anything I said, merely nodding when I spoke. As a result, I said less and less, until, by the time I left, I was spending eighty euro an hour to sit in a room in silence, trying not to make eye contact with the man sitting opposite me. A psychiatrist I saw monthly prescribed me antidepressants but did not talk either. My regular doctor had been trying to persuade me for months to take a break from work, and, eventually, I agreed.

I arrived home the evening after accepting the doctor's letter, and, too embarrassed to call my boss, sent a text message to let him know that I would be off for two weeks.

I sat the phone aside and headed upstairs. Martha was eating on the roof garden. Turvy was batting a long, viney stem that dangled over the side of a potted plant. Martha looked up and smiled at me, nodding, gesturing that her mouth was too full to speak. I sat across from her at the pink metal table. When she'd swallowed what she was eating, she pointed at her bowl and said, "Want some? It's pea and mint soup. The mint is from one of these plants."

I shook my head. "No. But thanks."

I looked out, beyond the wall of the roof garden. The neighborhood, until the Irish economic boom, had been characterized by poverty and drugs. Now in 2005, at the height of the boom, there were young professionals – from the media and arts, mostly – amongst the old-time inhabitants, but, apart from a shiny new Italian restaurant at the corner of the road, the area looked the same. The view was of rows of narrow, badly-designed houses, separated by alleyways full of rubbish – heaps of black plastic rubbish bags, often torn apart by skinny cats – awaiting the weekly bin collection day.

I turned back to Martha and said, "I'm going to be home from work for a couple of weeks."

She looked up. "Oh? Why?"

I lifted a paper napkin from the table and folded it in half in a triangle, then folded it in half again. I began, unable to say it directly – *I'm depressed* – "I haven't been sleeping well, like I've told you. The doctor –" I looked away. "The doctor thinks it's depression. I don't know. I've been seeing a therapist and going to group therapy. It hasn't helped. I've started taking medication, but only recently, and it might take a few weeks to take effect. In the meantime, the doctor thought a break from work would be good."

Martha had stopped eating. Her eyes were distant, then she turned to me. "I'm sorry to hear that. I know what you mean. I used to have depression. I mean, maybe I still do, but I feel OK now from the meds. I've had it since I was nineteen. It took until a couple of years ago to find a medication that helped."

I nodded, surprised. She was cheerful, always; funny, upbeat. "And you feel OK now?"

She shrugged. "I'm better than I was."

A month later, I sat across from Martha, and she pushed the plunger of the coffee-pot down with both hands. She poured coffee into two cups the size of bowls. Topsy sat on her lap and rubbed his head against her chin. I pulled my robe tight. It was late summer now, and a chill was beginning to creep in. I had returned to work, fuzzy and numb from the antidepressants, but still not sleeping.

I took my coffee. Martha coughed then began, "My antidepressants are no longer working."

I stared at her. "I'm sorry to hear that." I sipped coffee from the cup, and waited for her to continue.

"I've exhausted almost all the drugs they have to offer me now." She scratched Topsy's chin. He purred loudly. "So I've started seeing a therapist."

I nodded. "Is it helping?"

Martha laughed, her expression rueful. "Not really. I go to the psychiatric hospital because that way, my medication and therapy are free. I was already on the waiting list for a free therapist. It took one and a half years to get one. And then they give me this woman – she's really not very good. She told me I should watch some *Frasier* to cheer myself up."

I sniggered. "You're making this up."

"No!" Martha almost shouted, causing Topsy to jump suddenly from her lap. "I'm not kidding. That was her advice. But the first time I saw her, I didn't trust her. She was wearing lilac fake Ugg boots. Can you imagine? Lilac!"

I smiled.

"And long flowing skirts. She would come in and sit down like this –" Martha stood up and sashayed across the room, rearranging her hair and skirt elaborately before sitting down.

I laughed. "You're going to keep seeing her?"

"I can't afford to see anyone else. I mean, *she's free.* Although I'm starting to wonder if she does more harm than good. The time she told me I just needed to watch more *Frasier,* I cried all the way walking home. I felt horrible, like there was nothing really wrong me. I just needed to watch more half-hour sitcoms – to *cheer up.*" Martha poured more coffee for herself and after checking my cup, for me.

"My psychiatrist," I told her, "doesn't say anything at all. She just hands over the pills. But I'm glad she doesn't speak. She has badly-bleached hair – like *trashy* bleached hair, and wears iridescent pink lipstick and leopard-print stilettos." I grimaced. "I shouldn't stereotype. Maybe she's a really good doctor."

Martha smirked. "One time," she said, "I was describing something to my therapist - it was something that had really upset me, and I began to cry, and she just looked at her watch and said 'OK, Martha, our time is up.' Then she stood up, and I swear, *yawned,* and said 'I'm on holiday next week, so we'll see each other the week after. Goodbye!' I was still crying, and she looked so *relieved* that the session was finally over, and she could get me out of the room."

Martha stood and pulled her hair up into an elastic that she'd been wearing around her wrist. She turned to me. "Never trust a therapist in lilac furry boots." She walked to the fridge. It was covered in postcards and pieces of notepaper, magneted to the door. "I'm going to make us both dinner tonight." She pulled out the vegetable drawer. "Grilled halloumi cheese –" She looked to the counter and back to the fridge "– with pita bread and sweet chili sauce. We'll eat outside on the roof garden. And I think –" She rooted in the back of the fridge "yep, we still have this bottle of white wine."

I finished the coffee, then asked her, "And why do you think it – the depression – has come back?"

Martha closed the fridge door, then looked to me. "I don't know. Nothing really. It's just – I don't like working from home anymore. That's all." She laid out the food and began to prepare our meal.

By autumn, Martha wasn't working at all. On a bright morning in early November, she came into my room. She sat down, breathless, on the bottom of my bed and waved her hands. "I have to tell you something."

I stared at her, then pulled the earplugs from my ears. "What is it?"

She shook her head, laughing, then leaned forward and buried her face in my feet at the bottom of the quilt. Still holding the quilt, she looked up. "I dreamt. Oh my God – ewww."

She pulled the quilt up over her face.

I stretched, sat up, and fixed a pillow behind my back. "Tell me!" I tugged at the quilt.

She sat up. "So – my new therapist? The one I started seeing last week? The one who looks like – "

She buried her face in the quilt again.

She was laughing, her laughter muffled. "What's wrong with me?" She looked up.

"The one who looks like Freud."

She nodded. "So, in my dream, I can't remember what happened, but I'm standing in front of him –"

She shook her hands out in disgust. "I was standing in front of him – and masturbating. Oh my god. What do you think it means?"

She leaned forward, burying her face again in my feet and shaking her head.

I brought my hands to my mouth and laughed. "No! You should tell him. You have to. Just say, 'So I had a dream I wanted to discuss with you,' and he'll nod," – I nodded gravely to demonstrate – "and say, 'please go ahead, Martha,' " – I gestured in a manner I imagined Freud might – "and sit back and smile patiently. And then you tell him,"

"Stop!" Martha raised her hands, laughing. "Stop!"

"And you'll say, 'Well, Dr... Dr' – is he – oh my god!'"

Martha nodded, laughing too much to speak.

"Dr Love? He's Dr *Love*?"

Martha pummeled the quilt, laughing. "Stop!"

"Well, Dr *Love*, last night I dreamt I was standing before you and," – I spoke coyly – "you know, *touching* myself." I paused. "Doctor, what do you think it *means*?"

Martha pulled herself from the bed. "Oh God, I'm sick. Really. Maybe I should tell him. He's so serious. He just sits there, with his beard, and his bookcases, and his glasses, like a *cartoon* psychiatrist. I would love to tell him. Just to see his reaction. That alone would be worth what he's charging."

She caught her breath and shook her coat out, still smiling. We stayed silent for a moment. Scraps of light from the broken slats in the wooden blinds were scattered across the floor.

Then she said, "But that's not why I'm here. Would you like breakfast? Eggs Florentine?"

I nodded and smiled. "Thank you."

Martha stood up and pulled up her coat from the floor. It was a deep purple. She wriggled her arms in and knotted a red woolen scarf around her neck.

"Are you going out?"

She nodded. "To buy spinach. And the newspaper."

"I'll make coffee while you've gone."

"No, no." She straightened the edge of the quilt where she'd sat. "No, I'll make it when I come back. I'll bring you breakfast in bed."

When she'd shut the door, I sank into the bed again and pulled the quilt up. It was a patchwork quilt that my grandmother had made twelve years earlier for my eighteenth birthday. *To give to your own children.* I felt something at the bottom of the bed and pushed it towards my hand with my foot. It was a punched-out blister pack from the sleeping tablets I took every night. I tried to remember. I had taken one before going to bed, and then, frustrated, another when I woke at 2am and was unable to return to sleep. I must have punched out the last pill and then fallen asleep with the empty packet beside me. I was becoming immune to the pills and needing more and more each night to sleep. Even with them, I woke after two or three hours, my heart racing, consumed with anxiety. I threw the punched-out packet in the wastepaper basket beside the bed then lay down again, closed my eyes, and waited for Martha to return.

A morning later that month, Martha wheeled her bicycle out from the hall to cycle into town. When she returned, I was sitting with a newspaper at the kitchen table. She didn't speak but walked past me to hang her bicycle helmet by the window and walked out quickly again. I called after her. "Mart?"

She didn't answer. I walked up to the hall. She was pulling her bag from the bicycle basket. She didn't turn around. I touched her arm. "Mart?"

She brought her hand to her eyes. I turned her around to face me. She wouldn't look up. I pulled her into my arms, and she dropped her head onto my shoulder, crying noisily now. When she pulled away from me, her face was swollen. She shook her head.

"I just got back from seeing him. Dr *Love*. I thought maybe, finally, this one would help. But he's just like all the others. He wants to talk about my childhood, and I don't want to talk about it anymore. I just – I know why I feel this way, but I need help feeling better. That's all."

She pulled herself away from me and lifted her bag from the floor beside the bicycle.

"I just need to lie down for a bit." She walked past me and up to her bedroom, stepping over the cat stretched out on the stair.

Two weeks later, Martha called me at work. She said, "My parents have persuaded me to come home for a while. They don't think it's good for me to be at home all day by myself when I feel like this. They're coming by this afternoon to pick me up. I'm not sure how long I'll stay there – just until I feel better. I wanted to ask if you'd mind looking after the cats? I'll leave you money for food."

"Of course," I told her and asked her to call me in a couple of days and let me know how she was.

A few days before Christmas, I phoned Martha and told her I would be gone until just before New Year.

"What should I do about the cats?"

"Oh." Martha sounded like she'd forgotten about them. "Can you see if Rita next door is going to be there? Then if you give her enough food for the time that you'll be gone, she can feed them on the roof garden."

On the bus to my parents' house on Christmas Eve, I sent Martha text messages, ostensibly from the cats.

"Come back! We miss you. It's not the same here without you at all."

"Have a purrrrfect Christmas, love Topsy and Turvy xx"

I returned two days before New Year. I sent Martha a message to tell her I was back. She replied only with "Ok. Thanks."

On New Year's Day 2006, Susan, a friend I knew through Martha, called. She had never called me before. She was crying. She told me, her voice incredulous, "Martha's killed herself."

I slid down to the floor against the wall. I said, "No, no," over and over, then, interrogating her, "But how do you know? When? What happened?"

"Today. Her parents went out for a walk and came back and found her dead."

"But how?" I asked her. I was shaking. It didn't make any sense. How could they go out for a walk and come back to find her already dead?

"I don't know. That's all I know. They asked me to call her friends. They just couldn't face it. Can you call me back tomorrow?"

I climbed onto the bed, crying frantically, unable to catch my breath. I cried most of the night, sleeping on and off and waking to the memory, but disoriented, confused. It was impossible. It had to be a mistake.

I called Susan in the morning. I fumbled, my hands shaking, trying to key in the digits. I waited for her to tell me that there had been a huge misunderstanding.

She said, "I spoke to Martha's parents." Then stopped, her voice choked.

"What did they say?"

"They went for a walk yesterday morning. They asked Martha to come along. She said, no, she was going to go for a cycle. When they came back–" Susan broke down.

I stayed silent.

"Martha had hanged herself from a tree in their garden. They found her body there."

Susan spoke fast, crying, sounding confused. "She sent me a Happy New Year message the night before! You know we were taking swing dance classes? I sent her a message wishing her a happy new year, and she wrote back saying – I'm going to read it to you – *Happy new year to you too! Look forward to swing dancing our way through 2006!* Why would she write that? Look forward to *swing dancing* our way through the year? Then do this the next morning?"

That evening, I went up to Martha's bedroom. Topsy was sleeping on her bed. I lifted him off. He miaowed indignantly. I carried him to the roof garden, dropped him onto the decking, and locked the cat flap. He pushed it and cried, annoyed. I sat back on Martha's bed. Turvy came to the door, and I shut it. He yelped in protest. I didn't care. *Why were the cats still here and she wasn't?* I lay back on Martha's bed. The room smelled of lemon oil she'd been burning in an incense burner. The pillow smelled of lavender, sprinkled onto the pillow-case to help her sleep. I held it tightly and cried.

The funeral was held five days later. The crematorium was packed. We stood three-deep against the wall. A crowd stood outside when there was no room for anyone else to come in. A Nick Drake song played when Martha's father and brother and other men I didn't know carried her coffin in. They walked slowly. Martha's father's face was contorted in pain. I tried to imagine carrying my child's coffin – my child who had ended her own life. I felt angry at her for doing this to him. I felt angry at the lilac-Ugged therapist for not taking her more seriously: couldn't they have admitted her to hospital, kept her on suicide watch? I felt angry at myself: I should have helped her more. The men lay her coffin on a platform at the front of the room. Untied flowers were strewn over the steps. At the end of the ceremony, the Beatles song, "Blackbird" began to play and the curtains on the platform closed slowly, the coffin behind them. It was the last time we would see it. I cried, holding my mouth closed, afraid I would howl.

When I returned home, I picked up the mail that had arrived in my absence. A bill addressed to Martha; stupid things that seemed cruel now: envelopes announcing "You're a winner!"; the latest copy of Vogue. The cats, hungry, ran down the stairs and miaowed at my feet. I shouted at them, shooed them away with the bunch of letters in my hand. I sat down in the kitchen. One of the cats batted something at the front door so that it sounded like it was being unlocked. I thought, *Oh, she's back. Of course. It was all a mistake.* Then silence, until the cats ran into the kitchen and miaowed again.

I looked around the room, at the furniture I had fallen in love with when I'd first visited the house, at the stack of magazines and scrapbooked recipes, at the old silver tray. I felt consumed with anger again. Why had she left me here alone, to feed her cats and pick up her mail? I let my head drop into my hands and sat, ignoring the cats' cries.

There was a sudden clatter, and I opened my eyes and looked up. Topsy had found an old piece of cheese that had missed, or fallen out of the trash can. Turvy was moving towards it, and he hissed and clawed at his face. When Topsy had eaten the cheese, both cats turned to me and cried. I stared at them, then stood, finally, and pulled open the bag of dry food that Martha had bought at the corner shop with me just before Christmas. The cats hadn't been fed since the morning before. I dumped some food in their bowl, tipped the old water from their drinking bowl out, refilled it, and sat down as they pushed each other out of the way to get to the food, crying, confused, afraid.

I stayed in Martha's house for six months after her death, collecting her mail to give to her parents, feeding the cats, resenting them, and helping to pack up her things. Her parents wanted to sell her house to have it off their hands as soon as they could. They couldn't sell it without a death certificate, and this couldn't be issued without a coroner's report, which took several months as any suspicious circumstances in her death had to be ruled out. There were issues too with her life insurance: her depression, the cause of her death, was a *pre-existing condition* – she had suffered from it since she was nineteen – but it hadn't been declared on her insurance application.

Martha's parents were filling their time with distractions in a way that seemed frantic and desperate. They were planning trips to Europe – hiking, ski-ing! – with friends. Her father was taking baking lessons. I would bump into them at cafes, at the cinema. They were seeing a lot of interesting films, they told me – *did I know there was an over-55 film club?*

Every Saturday, they would come to collect Martha's mail, and I would make them breakfast. They would compliment me, say they would love the recipe for my pancakes, though I had made them with mix from a box. They would tell me about the movies they had seen since we'd last bumped into each other at the cinema. We sat in the kitchen, surrounded by Martha. The plants she had nurtured that I was slowly allowing to die. The cats that I now hated, unreasonably, and other than feeding, ignored. The old green armchairs that she had rescued from a skip. The pictures, stack of Vogue magazines, the cooking scrapbooks, the books. Her parents would talk – about holiday plans, about films, about baking – without pause. It made me nervous, uneasy. I felt that if they stopped, they would come apart along the seams of their grief.

Later, when they came, they began to seem less frantic and more broken. They talked less of plans for travel and took Martha's mail from me absentmindedly, fingering the clear envelope window that displayed her name and address. They seemed bewildered that the mail – junk, most of it – continued to come, that she still wasn't there to pick it up. That there was just me, someone they hadn't even known a year earlier, living in their daughter's home.

Martha's house, and my life, began to feel contaminated, diseased. I felt like suicide was *catching*. I became afraid to stay there. It felt like depression had gotten the better of one of us, and that if I didn't leave, I might succumb too.

I scanned papers and websites for jobs overseas. I found a post in human rights education at UNESCO in Namibia. The Irish Government was funding it through the UN Volunteer (UNV) program. UNVs were not truly volunteers but received a living allowance. The Government was trying to meet a target of 0.7% of GDP spent annually on aid. Finding ways – good ways – to spend this much was, it turned out, harder than it seemed. Sending Irish staff to already-existing UN offices and paying them a UNV allowance was one of the easier ways to get closer to the target.

I applied for the position and was accepted. Soon after, the Irish Aid office told me that UNESCO had changed the terms of the post, and it no longer had anything to do with human rights. It seemed that they had seen an opportunity – free staff from the Irish Government – and created a post simply to conform with Irish Aid's human rights and humanitarian criteria. Once the free employee was confirmed, they changed the job description to general administration. "They want," the man at Irish Aid told me, "a free employee to do whatever they need. That isn't what we want to fund."

A week later, Irish Aid called me again. Now they had an opportunity to fund a post for a protection officer at UNHCR, the UN refugee agency. Could they send the office in Kampala my CV?

Five years earlier, just after leaving Prague, I had spent nine weeks traveling alone in East Africa – in Malawi, Mozambique, Tanzania, and Zambia – but I had never been to Uganda, and never worked in Africa at all. I also had no experience working with refugees. I was shocked then, when the office called me back the next morning to say I'd been accepted, to start as soon as I could.

I wondered whether I would be taking a job from a local person who could do it better than I could. But then, this job wouldn't exist if the Irish Government weren't sponsoring it. Could I do something useful? Would I feel more worthwhile than I did now? I thought back to visiting the UNHCR office in Bosnia years earlier, and how that had set me on this path. There was an appealing sense of destiny to the offer, coming so out of the blue.

I called Irish Aid back just hours later and said I would take the post.

On the day I was due to move out, Martha's parents came by to say goodbye. They had brought the framed picture, *Flower Paintings,* with them, having already taken it to their house with much of Martha's other possessions.

"We wanted you to have it," Martha's father told me. I had already explained that the picture was the main reason I had come to see the house – that it was responsible for me becoming part of Martha's life.

"Something to remember her by."

They handed me a card, written as though from the cats. *Thank you for caring for us so well! Love Topsy and Turvy.* I felt momentarily overwhelmed with guilt, remembering them crying at the cat flap or the bedroom door, after I had locked them out.

My father came to pick me up, to drive me and my boxes to my parents' house. I would stay there for a week, then leave the country completely. At the beginning of July 2006, I would take a series of flights from Dublin to Entebbe in Uganda, the country where I would be based, according to the terms of the post, for the next two years.

III. Tell Me Why You Fled

Jesus is Merciful Hairdressing Saloon

On the plane to Uganda, I rehearsed the conversation I would have with the driver who would pick me up at Entebbe Airport, the questions I would ask him – about the country, refugees' lives, the UN. When I saw him at Arrivals however, he was yawning, bored. He threw my backpacks into the trunk of the white UN Landcruiser, the first I had been in since my trip to Bosnia in 2000. Then he opened the back door and tossed in the placard that bore my name in blue marker capitals, sloping downwards, misspelled.

The sun was coming up as we pulled out of the airport. The dirt paths on either side of the road to Kampala were thronged with people. Men and women in suits appeared to be walking to work, adolescent boys transported goods on the backs of their bikes, and women carried improbable loads – stacks of wood, sacks of grain – on their heads. Children in school uniforms held hands, laughing, and tripped on their flip-flops, which were often too large. Women sat by the side of the road with baskets heaped with avocados or small, stumpy bananas or pyramids of tomatoes on mats on the ground. Other women sold strips of phone credit. Small wooden shacks bore hand-painted signs: *God's Grace Mobile Phone Repairs. Jesus is Merciful Hairdressing Saloon.* Chickens ran, squawking, into the street. It felt chaotic, and I suddenly felt jubilant, alive: *I am here.*

We arrived in Kampala, and the driver dropped me at a hotel close to the building of the UN Development Program, UNDP. A room had been reserved for my first night, and I would receive a stipend to stay there for up to a month while looking for an apartment or a house.

The hotel was a low-slung building that featured a desk in the hallway – no reception – and one long corridor of rooms. I hauled my backpacks into my room. The bed was narrow with tightly-pulled white sheets and a gaudily-patterned fleece blanket. The mosquito net was dirty and torn. I turned on the fan. It didn't work. I flicked the light switch and realized that the electricity wasn't working at all. I cranked the window open. Even in the city, it smelled like the tropics. I untucked the edges of the mosquito net, lay down, and breathed it in.

My first two weeks consisted of orientation at the offices of UNDP. The office was centrally located, and I spent my lunch hours and evenings before sundown exploring Kampala on foot.

The city spread, untamed and green, over hills on the edges of Lake Victoria. It was lush with banana plantations, and the plump fruit of mango trees dotted the red dirt earth. Tall, skeletal marabou storks – known as "undertaker birds" because of their black wings, white chests, and hunched stance – picked through garbage downtown. Children played in slums, chasing tires with sticks. Ubiquitous boda-boda motorbike taxis dodged cars and death. They rarely carried only one passenger – more often there were two people balanced behind the driver, sometimes a whole family, sometimes a woman with a baby tied to her back. I saw a boda with a dead cow strapped to the back seat. Even coffins – containing bodies – could, I would learn, be transported this way.

In the weeks leading up to my departure, I had read as much as I could about Uganda. The country was a British protectorate from the late 1800s until 1962, and English was still an official language. School lessons were taught in English, so everyone who had attended at least a few years of primary school could speak it. The infamous dictator, Idi Amin, had seized power following a military coup in 1971. During the eight years of Amin's rule, an estimated 300,000 Ugandans lost their lives at the hands of his regime. The Indian community, originally brought by the British to East Africa to build the railway, was forcibly evicted. At the time of their ousting, many owned large businesses or had professional occupations in Uganda, and their eviction had devastating effects on the economy.

The current president of Uganda, Yoweri Museveni, had, by 2006, been in power for twenty years. Joseph Kony's Lord's Resistance Army – the LRA – had been terrorizing northern Uganda for almost the same length of time. Around 1.8 million people had been displaced by the LRA, and many lived in squalid conditions in camps for internally displaced persons – IDPs. The LRA had abducted thousands of children, and routinely raped women and girls.

UNHCR was, I read, tasked with assisting IDPs in Uganda as well as refugees, but I would, according to my terms of reference, only be working with refugees: those who had fled to Uganda from other countries.

Though conflict persisted in the north of the country, Kampala, where I would be based for the duration of my post, was apparently safe.

The coordinator for the UN Volunteer program through which the Irish Government had sponsored me, was based at the UN Development Program (UNDP) office. His name was Emmanuel, and he was charged with providing the orientation I would undergo before beginning work at UNHCR.

Emmanuel was Tanzanian and aged somewhere, I couldn't determine exactly where, between twenty-five and sixty. He wore, in spite of the heat, a buttoned-up polyester suit. His shirt was neatly ironed, and he wore brass cufflinks and potent aftershave. Though he himself was in fact only a UNV, he gave the impression that he ran the entire operation.

My orientation mainly entailed filling out forms: forms for annual leave, sick leave and home leave; and of completing a CD-ROM on "security in the field." The CD-ROM consisted of lessons on security precautions: how to identify a landmine; how to choose the safest room in a hotel; how to find your way home after being kidnapped, using only the stars. There was a short, interactive quiz at the end of each lesson. In my favorite quiz, a tiny UN Landcruiser moved further along a path out of the jungle to safety with each correct answer. Every wrong answer sent it hurtling back.

On the last day of my orientation, Emmanuel called another Irish UNV, Rachel, into the office. Rachel, like Emmanuel, worked for UNDP. "Rachel is looking for a roommate," he told me. "Maybe you could move in with her? What do you think, Rachel?" He took her hand and smiled at her in a way that implied she would do well to take his suggestion on board.

When Emmanuel finally looked away, Rachel rolled her eyes and shook my hand. She told me she was going home an hour later, and I could share a taxi to her house.

Rachel lived in the former servants' quarters of a property belonging to a Ugandan man named Edgar. The servants' quarters was a two-bedroom cottage across from the main house. The main house, where Edgar lived with his wife, children, and actual servants, was large and imposing. The windows of both houses were barred for security. The high walls around the garden were topped with razor wire. A guard stood in a small concrete hut at the front of the garden. It was his responsibility to keep out intruders and open the gate for the family, servants, and visitors.

Edgar had bought the property with money he'd made working in security in Iraq. All over Uganda, I had just learned, men were being recruited by American security contractors, like Blackwater, operating in Iraq. The work was extremely dangerous, but many Ugandans were still agreeing to go. A few days after I arrived, a taxi driver had told me he was contemplating it, and I asked him why. "For the money," he said, shrugging his shoulders. "There's nothing I could do in Uganda to earn nearly that much. If I go, and I survive, I can come back and build a house for my family, give money to my parents. It's more money than I could earn in a lifetime here."

"How much do the security companies pay?" I'd asked, trying to imagine the price for which he was willing to risk his life. He raised his eyebrows as though I wouldn't quite believe it, and would immediately understand the temptation: "$1,000 per month."

Later, I would look up what Americans were paid to do the same work: around $1,000 a day.

A week after seeing Rachel's house, I checked out of my hotel. Upon checkout, the receptionist asked me, baffled, "Why did you never have your room cleaned while you were here?"

I was confused. "But no one came to clean it." When I arrived back the first evening to discover that my room hadn't been cleaned, I assumed that room service simply wasn't part of the deal.

She looked at me, as though wondering if this was my first time to ever stay in a hotel. "But you have to give us the key when you want your room cleaned – we only have one key per room. You – what? Took it with you each day."

I didn't know how to respond to this. No one had told me that I had to hand in my key. I said, "I'm sorry," as though, somehow, I was the one who had put the hotel out. The receptionist nodded at my apology, as though she would let it go, but only just.

I had gone to work hungry for my first week too because I had no idea that the hotel did, in fact, serve breakfast, in a veranda across a courtyard from the building with the bedrooms. I used travel-size Kleenexes for toilet paper for days before summoning up the nerve to tell the front desk that I'd run out.

I had gone without toilet paper – and breakfast and clean sheets – rather than risk looking like the pampered, naïve, new white girl in town.

Rachel invited me for drinks with her colleagues on evenings after work, and I met a few other expats living in Kampala. From their conversations, I understood that they all had several Ugandan staff working for them. They discussed the meals their cooks had made, complained about the quality of their cleaners' and gardeners' work, and called their drivers to pick them up from the bar. I felt proud that I was renting a room in the servants' quarters of a *Ugandan's* property. I began to drop this fact casually into conversations with other expats: the subtext of my situation being that I was different – more thoughtful, less spoiled – than all the other *mzungus* – white people.

My accommodation in the servants' quarters did not, however, go as planned. A month after I moved in, Edgar decided that since there were now two of us – me and Rachel – living there, he would double the rent. We were outraged. It didn't make sense! The house was still the same size – and wasn't it that on which the rent was based? We fought Edgar, pointing out the lack of logic in his decision, but he wouldn't give in. We shook our heads.

"If," Rachel said wearily, "he wants Westerners to rent from him, he's going to have to learn how it's done."

My pride in my living situation was replaced with confusion. I didn't understand why Edgar was so misguided and why he was so happy to let us go. It was hard to accept that the living situation about which I had been so smug, had come to an end in only a month.

But the living situation wasn't the only thing that threw me: my new work environment, it turned out, would confound me even more.

On Behalf of the United Nations

My colleagues at Amnesty International and the other NGOs where I had worked were, for the most part, devoted, and worked long hours for little pay. On work-related trips, they rode the bus and shared rooms in hostels, rather than using organizational funds for hotels. I had imagined my new colleagues to be an older, more experienced version of my MA class; or a more global version of the staff at the NGOs where I'd worked. I hadn't considered that the six-figure salaries earned by many international UN staff, and the lifestyle that came with the work in countries like Uganda – the servants, maids, drivers, cooks, and power – might attract other kinds of employees too, or corrupt those whose intentions were, at the outset, good.

My new boss was a man called Ali. He told me that he was forty-three, but he looked no younger than sixty. Though he had been born in Lebanon, and still spoke English with a heavy accent, he was a US citizen, having moved there when he was thirteen. He only ever referred to himself as American. He was single but had a girlfriend in New Zealand that no one had ever met. He was bald but tonsured, his hair at the sides longer than it needed to be. His skin was weathered from hot climates and access to cheap, developing-world cigarettes. He dressed in coordinated outfits that, we learned later, his mother had helped him choose.

During my first week at the office, my colleagues and I were invited to the wedding of Ali's secretary, Pamela. I had never met Pamela: since I'd started, she'd been off on official "wedding-planning leave."

Pamela, like most of the clerical staff in the office, was Ugandan. Lower-level posts in UN offices were filled by local staff; management posts were only open to internationals. If a Ugandan wanted to apply for a managerial post, he or she would have to look to an office in another country. This was the case worldwide, I had learned: clerical posts were open to locals, and higher-level posts were open to a pool of international staff, who rotated from country to country, usually spending a maximum of five years in one location, and being deployed periodically to UNHCR's headquarters in Geneva.

Pamela's wedding reception was to be held at a resort on the shores of Lake Victoria, about half an hour from Kampala. Ali offered to give me a ride. We would pick up three interns, who'd also just started at the office, at a junction along the way.

On the day of the wedding, Ali and I had almost reached the crossroads, when the interns called to say that they were on their way to meet us on boda-bodas, but had gotten lost. Ali pulled up on the side of the road and looked around. There was a desolate-looking bar just ahead, with plastic seats and tables in its car park. Ali called the interns back, described the bar, and said we'd meet them there. He parked and muttered, "Typical."

The bartender unfolded a parasol that was stuck through a hole in a table, and we sat down. Ali looked at his watch. I ordered a Ugandan Bell lager and asked if he wanted one. He ignored me and spoke to the waiter directly, requesting a mineral water, so long as it was cold. He got up, saying he needed to find a toilet. I lit one of his cigarettes while he was gone.

"Did the interns call?" he asked as soon as he returned. I inhaled deeply on his cigarette and shook my head.

"Then call them again."

I exhaled and pulled my phone out of my bag. When I got through, one of them, a twenty-one-year-old English woman named Claudia, said they'd returned to their house but would be leaving again very soon. I relayed this to Ali. He didn't say anything, then lifted his cigarette pack, and asked if he could take one. I looked at him, confused, for a moment, then said: "Sure, help yourself."

He pulled a match from the box by the cigarettes, tried and failed to light it, swore and threw the whole box of matches in the ashtray, then found a lighter in his pocket. I smiled and brought the Bell bottle to my lips. Ali pushed his sleeve up to look again at the time. "Did they say they knew where it was?"

"It seems they do."

Ali inhaled deeply and looked around. "I can't stand lateness. Or disorganization. Why didn't they plan in advance?"

I shrugged, smiling, as if to say, *Beats me.*

He put his cigarette out. "I come from a family of very organized people."

I nodded to emphasize my interest.

"I would never be late."

I smiled like that went without saying.

"My brother" – Ali stabbed the lighter at the table – "is one of the most organized people you'll ever meet."

I nodded again and reached for another cigarette. I offered Ali one. He impatiently shook his head. "My brother," he said, "is the kind of person who" – he cast around, as though looking in the car park for an illustration – "when his bank statements come, knows before opening them, the time, date, place and amount of every single transaction for the last three months."

I laughed. "Rainman."

Ali frowned. "Who?"

I shook my head. "It doesn't matter." I blew smoke out into the car park.

Ali looked again at his watch. I ordered another drink. We sat mainly in silence for the next half hour. The interns arrived, climbing off the backs of three separate boda-bodas. They greeted us cheerfully. I smiled back. Ali told them to get into the car, and we took off, not waiting for the change from our bill.

We arrived at the lakeside resort and said we were there for Pamela Masiko's wedding party. An Indian hotel representative brought us to a reception right on the lakeshore. Around six hundred people sat on chairs that were draped in white cotton with gold mesh bows tied around the backs. The bridal party sat on a sort of stage facing the crowd. The stage was elaborately decorated with white and pink flowers and draped in more gold mesh. African drummers and dancers stood along the edge of the lake. A wedding usher greeted us, and led us to a table at the front of the crowd, facing the bride and groom. We sat down, the interns looking relieved that we were finally there. The other guests at our table smiled, looking faintly bemused: we were the only white people amongst all of the guests. Waiters took our orders for drinks: everything, they told us, *was on the house*. The interns and I ordered gin and tonics. Ali ordered a whiskey and sat back.

I scanned the crowd for people we knew, but couldn't see our Ugandan colleagues anywhere. After a dramatic performance by the drummers, the speeches began. We downed our drinks, and within moments, they were replaced. Ali began to nudge me. I turned around, already tipsy.

"I forgot," he whispered loudly, "to write a speech. As Pamela's boss, I'll be expected to say a few words. Do you have" – he made a gesture of writing with his thumb and forefinger in the air – "a pen and paper?"

The first speaker finished, and everyone clapped. Some cheered. I searched in my bag. I passed Ali a leaky biro and a safari company business card. While the next person spoke, Ali wrote his speech in tiny writing on the blank side of the card. I gestured to one of the interns, a young student called Lars, and whispered, "Where's everyone else?"

Lars raised his shoulders as if to say *who knows?*

I felt the bride staring at us from her platform. I met her gaze. She didn't smile but narrowed her eyes. I sat back and sipped at my drink. The current speaker was thanking the VIPs in the audience for coming: the former foreign minister, royalty from elsewhere in Africa, those who'd flown from around the world to attend. I looked at the crowd, who were clapping respectfully at his acknowledgments. How was Pamela so wealthy and well-connected? And if she was so wealthy, why was she still working as Ali's secretary? The speakers each wished the couple luck, referring to them, for reasons that weren't clear, as Ronald and Masiko, the groom by his first name, and the bride by her surname. The gold-colored matchboxes on the table were similarly inscribed: *Masiko & Ronald.* The waiter returned, and we ordered more gin. I turned to Ali. He was still scribbling on the card, writing over the safari company's details on the other side now. I played with the tiny gold matchboxes. The speeches continued. Ali was reading his to himself now, mouthing the words, his face expressive, as though practicing to deliver it. The drinks arrived, and we lifted them, nodding to the waiter in thanks. He smiled graciously and left. The other guests at our table didn't look up; they hadn't ordered anything since we'd arrived. Another speaker walked to the front. I sat back with my drink. Everyone in the crowd was so much better dressed than we were. Ali wore his work suit, Claudia and the other female intern, a 24-year-old Canadian called Frieda, wore tank-tops and short floaty skirts, and Lars, a 22-year-old Swede, wore a linen shirt, sleeves rolled up, with khaki slacks. I wore a sundress and chunky wooden jewelry I'd bought at a craft market on my first weekend in Kampala. The other guests were in full celebratory regalia: headdresses and floor-length gowns.

I finished another drink and looked around for the waiter. I noticed, suddenly, that Claudia was laughing and covering her mouth. Lars and Frieda were biting their lips. Frieda tried to mouth something to me. I mimed that I didn't understand. Ali, sitting behind, was also nudging me. He leant over my shoulder and whispered: "I want to show you something."

I turned back to him and smiled, but then looked again to the interns. One was looking away, trying to stop laughing. I mouthed, "What?"

Then the next applause came, and Lars leaned towards me. "This," he whispered between almost choking, "This – is not our wedding."

Ali prodded my shoulder from behind. He said into my ear, "I need you to look at this now!"

I leaned forward and, confused, whispered to Lars, "Are you sure?"

He nodded, still coughing. Claudia was facing away, tears running down her cheeks. I looked around. We were the only white people in a crowd of around six hundred, downing free drinks at the front, sitting directly in front of the bride and groom. I bit on my thumb to suppress my laughter. Ali was nudging me urgently. I turned around. He passed me the safari card. I tried to make it out. It read, "On behalf of the United Nations, I would like to wish our valued colleague and her husband Ronald much happiness for the future. We are very honored to be here."

I was shaking now from trying not to laugh. I tried to see without turning whether the other guests at our table had noticed. Claudia had her head in her hands. Frieda was trying to look fascinated by the latest speaker. I turned back to Ali, and tried to whisper without laughing, "It's very good."

Ali asked, "Should I read it now?"

I shook my head, but couldn't speak. "You could, but – "

He raised his eyebrows, his expression earnest, "There's something wrong with it?"

I shook my head again, "No," and began to laugh and covered my mouth. "No, you can make the speech, but these people don't know us. This isn't our wedding."

Ali's mouth fell open. "What do you mean?" He looked up towards the stage. "That isn't Pamela?"

I said I didn't know Pamela, but no, it seemed it wasn't her. Ali peered at the bride.

"There are too many flowers obscuring her face. It's impossible to see her properly."

The flowers suspended from the stage ceiling stopped several feet above the bride's head. Ali sat up straight. "This isn't our wedding?"

I shook my head and turned to the interns. Lars whispered, "We received an SMS from Caroline – the filing clerk – wondering where we were. They're inside – in the hotel."

Ali was still making as if trying to see the bride. "I can't see her – are we sure it isn't her?"

Claudia nodded, wiping her face.

I said, "But you can still make your speech if you want – wish them luck on behalf of the UN."

Ali looked indignant. "Well, how are we going to leave?"

Frieda had regained self-possession. "We'll have to go one by one."

Ali objected, "But we're sitting right at the front! Facing the bridal table!"

"We'll have to go quietly," Frieda replied. "As though we have a reason to leave."

The crowd began to clap the latest speaker, and we sat up and joined in. Lars took advantage of the noise to lean forward and say, "I'll go first, and wait for you all by the car."

The clapping ended. The guests at our table made approving noises. We lifted our drinks. Lars made a show of taking his cigarettes from his pocket, waved them at us, and left. We sat on. When a suitable interval had passed, Claudia and Frieda left, saying loudly that they needed to use the bathroom.

I was left with Ali. We lifted our glasses to a speaker's toast. Ali sighed, did a little stretch, then got up and left. The guests at our table looked to the empty chairs. I smiled at them, then turned back to the speakers. Then I looked at my watch, and as if remembering something, stood up quickly, finished my drink, and left.

The others were waiting for me, the interns now convulsed. One, seemingly emboldened, asked Ali how he didn't realize it wasn't the right bride. Ali replied shortly, "I couldn't see her. There were too many flowers."

Claudia giggled. I said, "So, did Caroline say where the right wedding is?"

Frieda nodded. "Yup. In the events room in the hotel."

We followed the directions of a parking attendant and made our way to the events room. The interior was dark and modestly decorated. Our colleagues were seated; they were halfway through their meal. The interns ran to another intern and fought to tell her what we'd done. I heard only, "The other bride's first name was the same as Pamela's last name, so the person at the gate thought that was our wedding!"

The other intern looked confused.

Ali sat beside me, and a colleague leaned towards us and said, "You're late!"

Ali examined his napkin. The colleague pointed to a long table laid out with food and said we should serve ourselves. I walked over to the table, Ali following me, and lifted a plate. There were stainless steel trays of chapatis, boiled greens and matooke, and pots of stewed goat and chicken legs. I heaped them onto my plate. Ali shook his head. "The Karibu Club is only the restaurant in this country where I feel safe eating meat. I won't eat it anywhere else."

I opened my mouth but didn't say anything. The Karibu Club was an expat hang-out that was part of a hotel. It sold bland burgers and overcooked pasta. Ali arranged a dainty mound of chapatis and greens on his plate.

The best man waited for us to finish eating before commencing the speeches. He announced a list of people who would be called upon to wish Pamela and her new husband Frank well.

Ali sat up straight when he heard his name. He reached into his pocket and took out the card, then passed it to me and said, "Are you sure it's OK?"

I read the speech again, laughing and feeling drunk. "Sure," I said, and he lifted it and stood up. Then I pulled the card back from him and read it again. "On behalf of the United Nations, I would like to wish our valued colleague and her husband Ronald – "

"Frank!" I whispered, "Not Ronald, Frank!"

Ali snatched the card back, looked at it, and snapped, "I know."

I told the story of the Wrong Wedding to all the friends I had made in Kampala. We laughed: what had the other guests made of us, a group of unknown white people, crashing the wedding, drinking all their drinks, then leaving? What did the bride, who had narrowed her eyes at me, think of her white gatecrashers? How could Ali mistake a strange woman for his own secretary?

Then, one day a few weeks later, Ali called me into his office. I had just interviewed a Congolese refugee and his son. Ali asked me, skeptical, how I was certain the man was really the boy's father. He was concerned that this was a case of child trafficking. "If you saw them," I laughed, "You wouldn't have any doubts! The boy is the spitting image of his dad." It was true – the boy bore a comical likeness to his father – his mini-me. I opened the file in my hands, to show Ali the photos of the man and son as proof.

Ali looked up at me, his expression one of bewilderment. "But don't you think," he lowered his voice, "that black people are like Chinese people – they all look the same?"

I stared at him and then at the stapled-in photos of my client and his son. The boy's mischievous, half-scheming smile was just like his father's. I turned again to Ali. I thought back to Pamela's wedding, and his inability to distinguish her, his own secretary, from a complete stranger. I rolled the file into a tube and tapped it against my hand. I closed my eyes and imagined him making his congratulatory speech to the wrong wedding guests, or, in front of everyone, calling Pamela's husband "Ronald" instead of "Frank." I wished now that I'd let him. I pictured the bridal couple's reaction to a strange white gatecrasher wishing them luck *on behalf of the United Nations*. Smiling, I imagined, like the boy in the photograph, I nodded and left the room.

Kolo Touré

I spent my first days at the UNHCR office reading reports on the refugee situation in Uganda. The greatest number of refugees in the country were, I learned, from Southern Sudan. Others had fled the genocide in Rwanda, war in Somalia, and political persecution in Ethiopia. There were army deserters who could not return to Eritrea and people who had been persecuted because of their clan in Burundi. A large number of female refugees had fled sexual violence in eastern Congo.

The 1951 UN Refugee Convention defines a refugee as someone who is unable to return to their home country because of a well-founded fear of persecution on grounds of race, religion, nationality, membership of a particular social group or political opinion, and has not committed any crimes that would exclude them from protection. Refugee status is granted by the government of the country to which the person has fled, or by the UN. Once a person has been given refugee status, they have the right not to be forced to return to their country of origin. A person who has applied for, but not yet been granted, refugee status, is an asylum seeker.

The conflicts in some of Uganda's neighboring countries were so protracted and had generated so many refugees, that those fleeing them were given "prima facie" refugee status upon arrival, meaning that they were assumed to be refugees without having to undergo individual refugee status determination.

Those who were granted refugee status by the Ugandan Government were given residency in the country, but they could not legally acquire citizenship or vote.

Most refugees in Uganda lived in settlements – long-term camps – where they received a small amount of assistance: seeds, tools with which to build a shelter, and food when they first arrived. Some lived independently in towns and were known as "urban refugees." Only a tiny number of urban refugees received financial assistance from the UN, which in 2006 amounted to around forty dollars per single person, per month.

In theory, refugees had three possibilities for a "durable solution": integration in the country to which they had fled, voluntary return to their country of origin, or resettlement to a third country. Integration in Uganda was difficult for refugees, given that they could not normally become citizens there. For many, ongoing conflict and persecution in their home countries meant that returning was out of the question. This left resettlement to a third country, which usually meant the US, Canada, Australia, New Zealand, or somewhere in Europe. Fewer than one percent of refugees in Uganda were being resettled each year. But the alternatives: living long-term in a refugee settlement or in poverty in a city in Uganda, or returning to a country that was still unsafe, meant that resettlement was highly sought after. Given its desirability, it was a sensitive area. I had heard of cases in other operations of staff accepting money – and sexual favors – in return for putting forward refugees' names for resettlement. I had heard of people posing as other people in order to be resettled. Of families paying other families to pretend their child was theirs: so that the child, at least, could have a chance at another life.

I was assigned to work in resettlement soon after I arrived.

The refugees identified for resettlement by UNHCR were, in theory, the most vulnerable – those who had suffered the most trauma in their home country, or who were at most risk if they remained in Uganda. My colleagues interviewed clients who appeared to meet these criteria and, if they did, forwarded their cases to me or another staff member working in resettlement. My role was to interview these refugees, assess them further for resettlement eligibility and credibility, and write up arguments on their behalf to persuade resettlement countries to take them in. The resettlement countries would then make the final decision about whether to give them a permanent home.

Because, by definition, those selected for resettlement were those who had been through the worst experiences, or lived in the worst situations, the refugees I interviewed had some of the most devastating stories to tell. I developed various strategies for coping with hearing these stories. The first was to let myself believe that the stories I heard were somehow not actually true.

＊＊

Olivier was a Rwandan refugee, and one of my first clients. His wife and two sons lived in Russia, and he wished to be resettled there.

Rwanda had been a Belgian colony, and older Rwandans were still Francophone. Olivier's file told me that he spoke French, and since I did too, I wouldn't need an interpreter for our interview.

The UNHCR office in Kampala did not allow refugees on its premises. This struck me as strange at first, but as I learned more about the office and organization, it no longer seemed surprising.

Since they could not come into our office, we interviewed refugees at a local NGO, on the other side of town. The NGO's building was run down, and interviews took place in dilapidated rooms the size of cells.

Olivier came to our interview wearing a dated-looking soccer shirt from the British team, Arsenal.

"Are you a fan?" I asked as he took a seat across from me in the interview room.

He looked confused, and I pointed to the T-shirt. He followed my finger down with his eyes, then smiled, understanding. I had already met many Arsenal supporters in Uganda, and the soccer team provided a talking point for me and people with whom I otherwise had little in common. I didn't care about Arsenal, but my dad and Michael, my boyfriend in Dublin, were fans, and I had learned just enough to sustain a conversation about the team. Some taxi-drivers had Arsenal stickers on their cars, and I passed the journey talking about the team's recent performance, which I now made a point to follow. One driver that I got to know well said despondently of his new girlfriend, "She is a beautiful, God-fearing woman – but unfortunately, she is also a Manchester supporter." The woman's beauty and fear of God could not make up for her regrettable support for Manchester United.

I told Olivier that I could recite the names of the starting eleven of the Arsenal team, in alphabetical order of first name. Michael had taught me the list of names so that I could recite them to myself at night as a means of fighting my insomnia. Reciting them had become an unusual, if slightly underwhelming, party trick. Olivier raised his eyebrows in bemusement and told me to go ahead: *allez-y!*

He listened intently as I recited the names, then shook his head, his expression grave. "You made a mistake."

I stared at him. I had recited the list – to die-hard Arsenal fans – many times, and no one had ever told me I was wrong.

"Colo Touré," Olivier explained patiently, referring to a member of the team from Ivory Coast, "does not go between Ashley Cole and Dennis Bergkamp, because his name does not begin with a "C.""

I stared at him. "K? *Kolo* Touré?"

He nodded, then smiled.

I told him I would have to memorize a new list, and he laughed, shaking his head in mock despair.

We sat back, quiet for a moment, and I opened his file. The first page said that he was a Rwandan Hutu, with a Russian wife and sons. "How did you meet your wife in Russia?" I asked, looking up.

Olivier sat forward. "I went there to study under Russia's cultural exchange program with Rwanda." He paused.

I looked at him, not understanding, and gestured for him to elaborate.

He continued, "The program was a tool of the Cold War. Russia awarded scholarships to Rwandan – and other African – students to study in Moscow or Leningrad on the condition that the students return to their home countries and put in practice what they'd learned. It was a way to extend the reach of Soviet propaganda."

I nodded, trying to imagine. Had the African students converted to Communism? Did they care about that aspect of the program? Was it only a way to get a free education, a life in – more or less – Europe? I found it hard to picture African students living in the Soviet Union, being indoctrinated, with the expectation that they bring the lessons they had learned back home. How many countries had tried to gain control in Africa in different ways? I was learning that the Chinese Government was engaging in this now: funding Ugandan university courses, government buildings, roads, hospitals, engineering projects, and sponsoring Ugandan students to study in China. Chinese sponsorship of infrastructure, education, and politics was happening all over Africa.

"What was your involvement in the program?" I asked.

"I was granted a scholarship. I spent eight years in Moscow learning Russian language, culture, and politics."

"And what happened?"

Olivier smiled ruefully. "While I was there, I fell in love with a Russian woman, Valentina. We got married and had two children. I could not remain in Russia after my education: that was a requirement of the program. So I returned to Rwanda to work and save, with the plan that my wife and children would join me as soon as I'd made some money and built a home. That was in 1993."

He paused, gazing down. He smoothed a peeling letter "C" from the logo for the team's sponsor, *JVC*, across his chest. I typed up everything he had said on the laptop we used to transcribe interviews.

"By 1994," Olivier continued, "I had bought a small plot of land with the money I'd earned from working. My wife and children had made arrangements to join me later in the year. Then –" he breathed in deeply. "Then, of course, in April of that year, the genocide began. In August, after it had ended, I heard that my father had been arrested. Many Hutus were." He straightened the hem of his T-shirt. "I was arrested soon after."

During the Rwandan Genocide of April to August 1994, the Hutu militia group known as the Interahamwe, as well politicians, soldiers, and civilians, had killed almost a million Tutsis, and the Hutus who supported them. When a new Tutsi regime was installed in Rwanda after the genocide, many Hutus were imprisoned, some guilty, some not. Around two million Hutus fled Rwanda, fearing reprisal.

Olivier continued, "I was kept in prison for eleven years until my trial took place. No charges were brought against me, and so I was released in 2005.

I stopped writing. "Why were you imprisoned for eleven years without charge? Why wasn't your trial held earlier?"

He shrugged. "The huge number of genocide suspects, and the lack of legal capacity meant that it took a long time for trials to take place. Even now, twelve years later, there are a lot of prisoners whose cases still haven't been heard."

I nodded, unable to imagine enduring this. I could not understand why Olivier did not seem more resentful now as he described it. Was he just exhausted? Defeated? Resigned? I had already had another client whose husband had been imprisoned for ten years following the genocide. His family had prayed for his release throughout this time. Finally, no charges were found against him, and he was scheduled for release. His wife, my client, went to bring him home from prison. Shortly after they had left the prison, the reunited couple were stopped in their car by armed men. The man was dragged out of the car, shot and killed, and his body thrown on the road. The motives were unknown. The man's children were waiting excitedly to see their father for the first time in ten years. Instead, it was his body that was brought home. The story would continue to distress me, long after I heard it. To spend ten years waiting to see your husband or father only to have him killed on his journey home after he was finally released? The woman's hands had shaken as she'd spoken to me. She stared off, always, into the mid-distance. Her children sat, not moving, in silence, as she told their story.

"What happened to your wife and children in your absence?" I asked Olivier.

He spoke quietly. "I haven't seen them in thirteen years. My sons were five and three years old when I left. Now they are eighteen and sixteen. When I was in prison, they'd send me letters; now we occasionally speak by phone. I've missed all of their childhoods."

I exhaled deeply, causing the pages of my notebook to flutter at the corners. I typed up what he told me. "And your father?"

"He's still in prison in Kigali."

I looked to the clock on the wall. The driver would be leaving soon to bring other staff and me back to our office, and I needed to finish the interview. "I'm going to visit Kigali this weekend," I told Olivier, smiling. It was an inappropriate, pointless thing to say, but I felt compelled to say it, to bring the conversation back to the ordinary, to make a connection between us again before I left. The connections made through conversations about places, food, or football, felt essential in the darkness of these interviews. They brought humanity into the room when the stories told there had none.

Olivier smiled. "Do you need a place to stay in Kigali? You should stay with my friend."

I shook my head. "Thank you. I'm going with some friends. We're going to stay in a hotel." Two friends I had made – other expats working at NGOs – and I had already booked a room in the Hôtel des Mille Collines, the hotel whose owner had sheltered over a thousand people during the genocide. When those sheltering ran out of water, they drank from the hotel's pool. The hotel, and its role during this time, had been made famous by the film, *Hotel Rwanda*. It was hard to reconcile the events that had taken place there with the images of a regular four-star hotel I had found online – our accommodation for a weekend break.

"I'm looking forward to drinking Rwandan coffee," I told Olivier. The comment sounded inane.

He raised his hands, "But I have some here! I'll bring some the next time we meet."

Back at the office, I submitted an application to the International Criminal Tribunal for Rwanda with Olivier's name. I needed confirmation from them, as I did for every Rwandan who was at least seven years old when the genocide took place, that Olivier was not on their list of perpetrators.

A few days later, the Tribunal replied: Olivier's name was not in their database. I could proceed. I checked for his father's name out of curiosity. It was there. He was a Category One suspect, one of the highest-level prisoners: those who were suspected of planning and masterminding the genocide. He was suspected of being, in Rwandan genocide terminology, a *planificateur.*

Two weeks later, I arranged to meet Olivier again. When I called him into the interview room, he was carrying a huge Thermos flask, a disposable white plastic cup, and a small knotted bag full of sugar. He brandished the items proudly as he sat down. The coffee! I had forgotten. Olivier poured from the Thermos into the plastic cup. The coffee was as thick as gravy. I sipped it. It was bitter. I untied the knot in the polythene bag and tipped the sugar into the cup, shaking the cup to mix coffee and sugar together.

I thanked Olivier, and he smiled. "I had a good time in Kigali," I told him, setting the cup down.

He nodded. "What did you do?"

I thought: I'd visited the Genocide Memorial, stayed in the hotel where genocide victims had taken refuge, taken photos at a site of mass burials.

"I went shopping," I said.

Olivier looked surprised but continued. "What did you buy?"

"Hand-made purses, bags, and jewelry."

This was true: I had bought travel bags made from local fabric and necklaces made from bone. But that stop at a crafts stall had accounted for ten minutes of a weekend trip. The rest of the time, I'd spent engaged in what every white visitor seemed to do in Kigali: *genocide tourism.*

"And I bought coffee, of course." I forced a smile.

"Was it as good as this?" Olivier asked.

I took a drink from the plastic cup. I didn't know the right answer to that. I told him, "Not quite."

The genocide memorial I'd visited in Kigali was built on the site where over a quarter of a million genocide victims had been buried. Still, it felt detached from reality. It felt like a museum anywhere, with information about dates and places and events that could have taken place on the other side of the world. I could not connect the city I was visiting, shopping, and drinking coffee in with the typed-up descriptions of mass killings; with the thousands of bodies beneath our feet. The hotel too was a regular four-star Francophone African hotel: full of mustached Belgian businessmen drinking Primus beer, and sunbathing expats. I swam in the pool, unable to conceive of hundreds of people, terrified and dying from dehydration, resorting to drinking from it.

I opened the document with notes I'd made from my previous interview with Olivier. I lifted the plastic cup to my mouth and sipped as much as I could stomach at one time. I looked at Olivier. "What were you doing during the genocide? What was your father's involvement in it?"

"When I was in Russia," he began, "my parents were living in Kigali. When I returned to Rwanda in 1993, I saw them only once. I moved to Gisakura, where my brother had found me work. After the genocide began, my brother was told by Interahamwe to kill his Tutsi wife. He refused." He paused, tugging at a stray thread on his T-shirt. It was the same shirt, the old Arsenal one, as before. "My brother and I were then forced to watch his wife being murdered – hacked to death by machete." He brought his hand to his forehead, then let it drop. "And then I had to watch my brother being killed the same way."

I typed this up, letting the coffee go cold. "What happened then?"

"I fled on foot towards Congo," Olivier told me, "but when I reached the Rusizi river, I was attacked by Interahamwe and left for dead."

"How did you get as far as the river?"

Olivier shrugged. "There were constant checkpoints, but I showed my Hutu ID and didn't mention that I planned to cross the border. There were bodies along the road and in the river." He sighed. "I don't have a clear memory of being attacked, but the woman who found me told me I had been beaten with a spiked club. When I came to, I was injured and unable to cross the river, so I stayed hidden in a house with many others, both Hutu and Tutsi."

"How long did you stay hidden there?"

"Until the genocide ended. When it was over, I went to Kigali to see if my parents had survived. I reached their house but found it abandoned. Neighbors, who had just returned, told me what they'd heard."

Olivier worried the thread on his T-shirt again. He looked up. I finished writing and gestured at him to continue.

"They said that my father had been arrested, and my mother had been killed by the Tutsi Rwandan Patriotic Forces, whose incursion, as you know, had brought the genocide to an end." He sighed. "My neighbors told me that my father had been arrested on suspicion of helping to plan the genocide, but I never found out if those charges were true. I moved into my parents' house, and it was from there, late one night, that I was arrested. I was told I was suspected of taking part in the killing."

"Do you know why they arrested you?" I asked him.

He raised his eyebrows. "It was obvious. My parents had a nice house and a lot of land. A high-ranking official in the new government moved into the house and took over the land soon after my arrest. He had arranged my arrest so he could lay claim to my property while I was locked up."

I took a sip of the coffee, though it was no longer even warm, and added more sugar. I looked to my notes, then asked Olivier, "Can I read what I've written to you one last time before you leave to ensure I haven't made any mistakes?"

Olivier stayed silent as I repeated his personal details: date of birth – 1962; ethnicity – Hutu; religion – Catholic; wife and children – in Moscow; languages – Kinyarwanda, French, Kiswahili, Russian. A person reduced to biodata in a form. I read back his testimony of what had happened to him in 1994. When I'd finished, he nodded to signify it was correct.

I explained to him what we could do. I told him we'd try to help with documents for his travel to Russia, but it would take some time, perhaps several months. I leaned forward.

"I'm afraid you'll have to be patient."

Olivier stared at me and laughed. "I was in prison for eleven years without trial. I've waited thirteen years to see my wife and boys. You think I don't know how to be patient?"

I shook my head, embarrassed.

He smiled. "So that's it?"

I nodded. He reached across the desk and shook my hand, local-style: thumb over, thumb under, thumb over, demonstrating first, and cheered my attempt, as if to tell me he didn't want me to feel bad.

"Thanks for the coffee," I said, hurriedly downing the thick, cold, over-sweet remnants in the cup. I threw the plastic cup in a waste-paper basket in the corner, knotted up the sugar, and passed the bag and flask back to him. He told me where I could buy some, next time I was in Kigali.

As he turned to leave, he winked at me and raised his finger. "Don't forget. *Kolo* Touré."

I smiled and watched him as he left, clutching the Thermos and sugar.

I didn't know for sure if Olivier was innocent, but his name had been cleared by the Tribunal, and the story he had told me was consistent with his earlier testimonies, recorded in his file. Prolonged detention of Hutus following the genocide was not uncommon in Rwanda and did not necessarily indicate that a person had done anything wrong. No charges had been brought against him. If his father was guilty, that didn't mean he was too.

I thought about what he'd told me: his fleeing to the border, bodies everywhere around him, on the ground and in the river; the attempt to murder him with a spiked club; the murders of his mother and brother; the eleven years spent in prison, in another country, continent, from his wife and children. I tried to imagine it, but all I could see were images from a Hollywood movie: technicolor explosions, people running, screaming, with crying children in their arms. The people in the scene were people far away, remote, on TV, *not real*. I couldn't find a place for the man in front of me, who winked at me and cheered my awkward handshake and laughed at my *Colo* Touré and made me undrinkable coffee, anywhere in the scene.

The Housekeeper

After Edgar doubled the rent for his servants' quarters, Rachel and I searched for other places to live, and found, eventually, a two-bedroom house owned by a rich Indian couple in their fifties. The house was one in a compound of four, all owned by the Indian couple, and all inhabited by white women.

After President Museveni took power, some of the Indian community who had been expelled under Idi Amin had returned to Uganda. Those who had come back now owned many of the expat-oriented businesses in the country: supermarkets, apartment blocks, restaurants, hotels. Ugandans complained at how the Indians exploited them – that they treated them like animals and paid them very little. "Even the whites," a taxi-driver told me, "are easier to work for than the Indians. The Irish are OK, but the best of all are the Greeks." His opinion was passionate and rehearsed, and I imagined him ranking the different races and nationalities in his head, re-ranking them in the wake of particular experiences and interactions, promoting certain nationalities and relegating others.

Though the owners of the house had property in Uganda, they still spent most of their time in the UK. The house was dark and horribly decorated. The location wasn't as nice as that of Edgar's house. The rent was two hundred dollars a month more than even the new, double rent that Edgar was asking. But a perverse adherence to principle meant that we could not continue to rent from him.

The cleaner in the Indians' house was a man. The Indians referred to him as a "houseboy," but this word made me even more uncomfortable than the word "maid" (*why? Because it was worse for a man to be degraded than a woman?* The possibility that this was my reason made me wince), so I elevated him to "housekeeper." I never learned his name.

The housekeeper didn't sleep in servants' quarters. He slept in the garage, with the dogs who guarded the compound. His bed was a thin mattress on the ground next to bowls of yellowed, hardened rice – leftovers for the dogs. He had to clean all four houses every day and wash the laundry of four households by hand. I watched him do the laundry in the garden behind the houses. He washed the clothes in a plastic bucket, his body bent in a perfect right angle, his back ramrod straight from, presumably, years of transporting goods on his head. He scrubbed and rinsed the underwear of the tenants then pegged it on the line, or lay it carefully on the grass to dry. *Why don't they buy him a washing machine?* I wondered each day, though I knew the answer: why would they spend the money on an appliance when they could get the housekeeper to do it for a fraction of the cost? It's not like he, in a place where there he would be hard pushed to ever find other work, could object or *leave.*

When the laundry was dry, the housekeeper brought it to the garage to iron it. The underwear was ironed to within an inch of its life; the creases in jeans were razor-sharp. Then he folded each woman's clean clothes and left them in a neat pile on her bed. When I watched him doing the washing, I could never determine the system he had for keeping each person's laundry separate – and yet I rarely missed anything, or got clothing back that belonged to someone else. On the occasions I did, it was underwear, and always underwear that resembled something that did actually belong to me. A pale blue pair of underpants that looked exactly like mine, apart from a narrow frill at the band. A bra, the right size, and color, that just had an extra bow. This suggested he didn't have a system for keeping the laundry separate, but relied instead on visual memory, stumbling only when two items, similar in color and design, flummoxed him. I wondered what he made of the amount of underwear we had, and the pairs of silk underpants that would cost more, alone, than his month's wages.

He left the house spotless, mopped the floors, cleaned the toilet every day. We left all our possessions – all our iPods and laptops – strewn around. No one thought to hide anything. We knew that the Indian couple's punishment – firing him and calling the police – would deter him from stealing.

I moved out of the Indians' house after a short time, but Rachel stayed on. I left in part because of my discomfort at the housekeeper's situation, though I wasn't sure how my leaving would help him. I didn't give him a tip. I had planned to, but didn't see him on the day that I left.

Sometime after I left the Indians' house, I went to see a Ugandan psychiatrist when my prescription of antidepressants, which I'd brought over from Ireland, ran out. I told her I had problems with guilt.

"Guilt about what?" she asked, as though this one would be simple to resolve. I told her, as an example, about the housekeeper in the Indians' house, whom I'd never tipped. She shrugged. "Why don't you tip him now?"

I stared at her, not understanding. "How?"

"*Go back*," she said slowly, as though to a particularly dense child, "hand him the money, saying 'I forgot to give you this.' "

Soon after this appointment, I went to dinner at a restaurant opposite the Indians' house. The seating area was outdoors, the tables set amongst faux waterfalls and hidden speakers that played the sound of croaking frogs. The restaurant served the best Indian food in town. There was a rule against tipping individual waiters, but the waiter who had served you would corner you as you left, and beg you to give him the tip, and not add it to the bill. If you did that, he would explain, the Indian owners would keep the money, and it would never reach him.

Since my old house was just across the street, I thought about going to tip the housekeeper. I pictured myself arriving at the house, the housekeeper, bewildered, greeting me, handing him the money, unable to explain, and running off. I couldn't decide how much I should give him, and couldn't think how to explain it. The idea of showing up so long after I'd left made me cringe, and embarrassment outweighed my guilt. I left the restaurant, trying to forget about the housekeeper and the tip, and push my guilt from my mind. I tried to convince myself that things were not as bad as I thought – the logic of *but aren't those people happy in their own way?* It was one of the lies that I was trying to tell myself, in order to feel better about the inequality that I was surrounded by and benefitted from. It was a lie I had seen others try to tell themselves too. It was easier than doing something – even walking to the house across the street, and a few Ugandan shillings in hand, knocking on a garage door.

Elton Hercules John

On a Saturday afternoon in August 2006, Mario, a friend I had met through Rachel, called and asked me to meet him at a local bar, Blue Mango. Mario was an Italian who worked for an international corporation, and was gay.

Blue Mango had a laid-back vibe and was furnished with low bamboo sofas with fat sponge cushions covered in local fabric. It played expats-in-the-tropics favorites, like Bob Marley's "No Woman, No Cry."

Mario had arrived before me and stood to hug me when I came in. He was drinking a Kenyan Tusker lager, and I ordered one too. He clinked his bottle with mine. He asked how I was, nodded quickly when I answered, then passed me the newspaper he'd been holding under his arm. I sat my Tusker on the bamboo coffee table in front of our sofa and unfolded the paper. It was a local tabloid called *Red Pepper*. Mario reached forward and flattened it open.

"Have you seen this?"

I stared at the page he had opened it to. The headline read "Gay Shock!" Underneath were names and photos of men who were suspected, apparently, of being gay or bisexual. I scanned the pictures. It seemed they were all Ugandans. There was no one I knew. I lifted the bottle of Tusker again and sipped at it slowly while I read.

To a majority of us, straight thinking citizens, it is an abominable sin, actually a mortal sin that goes against the nature of humanity. We are talking about men in this nation who are walking closely in the footsteps of Sir Elton Hercules John and the like by having engines that operate from the rear like the vintage Volkswagon cars. To show the nation how shocked we are and how fast the terrible vice known as sodomy is eating up our society, we have decided to unleash an exclusive list of men who enjoy taking on fellow men from the rear. We hope that by publishing this list, our brothers will confess and go back to the right path.

I placed the paper on the bamboo coffee table in front of our sofa. I smirked. "Sir Elton *Hercules* John? Engines that operate from the rear?"

Mario smiled briefly but looked away. "I know some of the people in the photos from gay nights at clubs. One of them, I heard, has already lost his job. I've heard stories of arrests. The article just came out last week."

I couldn't believe that anyone took this seriously. I asked, "But who even reads this trash?"

Mario shrugged. "A lot of people, it seems. If they publish my name, I'll have to leave not just my job but the country." He took a large swig of his Tusker, and it bubbled over the top of the bottle as he brought it down. He stopped the frothing beer with his thumb. He said more loudly as if trying to reassure himself, "But I'm not suddenly going to change who I am."

I lit a cigarette and pulled an ashtray from the coffee table onto the sofa. The cushion covers were cream, with a pattern of blue elephants. It was a fabric that I saw everywhere: on furniture, curtains, even, to my amusement, on shirts. Sometimes, a person in a blue elephant shirt would be sitting on a sofa of the same pattern, as if in camouflage. I thought about the article. It was awful, especially the list of names and photos, but it was absurd. *Like the Vintage Volkswagon cars?* The language was laughable: sensationalist and crass. Did people really lose their jobs over this?

Mario drank the last of his Tusker, lifted the paper, and stood up. "I just wanted to show you that. I was upset when I read it but," – he smiled forcefully – "That's where we're living." He gestured to the photos of the "suspects." "Unlike these poor fuckers, I can always leave."

At work a week later, my colleague Patricia called me into her office. Patricia was a pale, freckled, Belgian woman, but she dressed in jewel-colored silk Pakistani saris. She'd bought them, I guessed, in her previous posting in Islamabad. She was one level below my boss Ali, whom she couldn't stand. They rarely spoke, and she made her disdain for him clear.

"I have a refugee I want you to interview," she said and passed a thick blue file to me.

Normally, files came to me from a clerk whose role was to assign them to resettlement staff. I didn't know why Patricia was giving me this file directly, in her office, with the door shut. The cover of the file told me the refugee was a Burundian man named Celestin, who had fled to Uganda in 2005. I opened it. As was standard, a passport photo was stapled inside. It showed a young man, perhaps still a teenager; fine-featured, with a vulnerable, faraway expression. I didn't understand. Patricia looked down at Celestin's photo, then back to me.

"I am bypassing the normal assigning procedures because I want you personally to take this refugee on."

I nodded, waiting. She slid the file back towards herself and traced the staple securing the photo with her finger, flicked through the pages without looking at them, then closed it completely.

She spoke quietly. "Some other staff members would refuse to work with him or be unwilling to argue his case."

I stayed silent, still not understanding.

She continued, "You know how they can be, sometimes."

I looked at the closed file. I had no idea what she was talking about. "I'm not sure what you mean."

Patricia opened the file once more and tapped at the photo with her fingernail. She said, "I'm pretty sure he's gay." She paused. "He could be in danger in Uganda if he is. As a refugee, he's already vulnerable, but there have been more and more attacks lately on anyone who's suspected of being homosexual." She traced the outline of the man's face in the picture. "I mean, he hasn't told us that he's gay – not yet – but interview him and see what he says."

I stared at the photo. "But how can anyone refuse to interview a refugee they've been assigned?"

Patricia sighed. "You haven't been here very long. Some of our colleagues – the more," she searched for the word, "evangelical ones, they don't want to work with a refugee who's been a prostitute, or had an abortion, or is gay. But," she gave a short laugh, "It's not like we have many refugees who admit to being gay, so this issue doesn't arise often. People will say anything to get resettled to the West – pretend they've been raped or lost children when they haven't – but even though being gay should be equally strong grounds for resettlement, they find it too shameful to say that."

I had already seen how what Patricia said was true: that many refugees were desperate to be resettled out of Uganda. And yet, though being gay was, in the context of worsening homophobia in Uganda, strong grounds for needing to be resettled, I hadn't heard of a client who admitted to this.

I knew too that many of my colleagues – of various nationalities – were religious. They sent chain emails to all staff: emails promoting worship of Jesus Christ that promised that those who forwarded them would come into a fortune or – my favorite – *lose weight*. I was shocked by the first one I received: I didn't understand how staff could send proselytizing emails, and chain emails with promises of rewards and threats, at the UN. That they could refuse to work with refugees because they were gay came as an even greater shock.

I took the file from Patricia and read through the notes that staff had made in earlier interviews with Celestin. They indicated that he was only nineteen and that his family were all missing or dead.

If Celestin really was gay, Uganda, it was becoming clear, was not a safe place for him to remain. It should be easy to persuade a resettlement country to take him in on these grounds. But what if he was too ashamed to admit to being gay? How would I argue his case then? I lifted the file and stood up. I told Patricia I would schedule an interview for the following week.

**

I had been told by senior UNHCR staff that when conducting interviews with refugees at the NGO's premises, I should sit on the chair closest to the door. The refugee should sit on the chair furthest from and facing the door, and there should be a desk between me and the refugee. This arrangement was, I was informed, in case the refugee became violent: then I would be able to back quickly out of the room.

The implication in this rule was that refugees were unhinged: animals, waiting to attack.

Celestin had delicate features and wore his hair in cornrows. His T-shirt was tight and stopped an inch before the waistband of his jeans. A faded image of a sun and palm trees and the words *Miami Beach Florida* adorned the front. His mannerisms were feminine, his voice soft and anxious. He spoke a little French, but his first language was Kirundi, so I interviewed him with the help of an interpreter. He told me his story, sometimes speaking behind his hands. He was Tutsi, he said, and had fled from Hutu rebels who had killed his father and brothers.

"Have you had any problems in Uganda?" I asked him quietly.

He shook his head and looked away.

I said, "I'm sorry, but I can only help you if I know everything that's going on."

He began to cry. The interpreter moved closer to him. We stayed silent for a moment, and Celestin wiped his tears with the back of his hand. I looked out the window: there was no one within view. For as long as I'd been in Uganda, no senior staff had ever actually come to the NGO's premises. I pushed away the desk that separated us and moved my chair beside Celestin's. Celestin turned to the interpreter and said something barely audible. The interpreter nodded slowly. He turned to me. "That priest who took him in, he violated him."

I looked to my notes: he was referring to the priest in Burundi who had sheltered him after his parents were killed. I said to the interpreter, "What do you mean, violated? Raped?"

The interpreter looked uneasy, then nodded.

I said, "I need to know when, and how many times."

The interpreter put my question to Celestin, and he began to cry again. I hesitated, put my hand to his arm, took it away, then put it back.

When Celestin spoke again, the interpreter told me, "You're the first person he's told about the rape. He finds it very hard."

I said, "It's OK."

Celestin had stopped wiping his eyes, and his tears fell to his shirt. He said it had happened three times before he'd run away, and there was another time: the man who had brought him from Burundi to Rwanda had raped him too.

I said I was sorry. I began to write, then put the pen down.

Celestin said, "No one knows this but you."

I nodded. "I know."

We didn't say anything for a moment, then I asked if he had any issues in Uganda. I needed information about the problems he had now to help my argument that he needed to leave. He shook his head. I put my hand to his shoulder and said we'd try to do what we could. "Courage," I told him in French – *hang in there* – as he stood to leave. He rubbed each eye with the heel of his hand and nodded, trying to smile. I left the room, not moving the chairs and desk back into place.

I shared my office in the UNHCR building with a Nigerian colleague, Rose. When I returned there, I told her about Celestin. I said that I wasn't sure if he was gay, and wished he would tell me if he was, so I could argue his case on those grounds.

Rose frowned, not looking up from her computer screen. "It's not God's way."

I stared at her. "Being gay? But how can he help that?"

Rose shook her head, still focused on the screen. "It's a choice he makes."

I leaned forward, though she still didn't return my gaze. "Why would he choose that? And why would he deserve to be persecuted even if he did?"

Rose flicked through a file on her desk. "I don't support persecuting him. But I will pray that he changes his ways."

I persisted, though she had stood to open a filing cabinet behind her now, and was rifling through those files. "Why should he change?"

Rose pulled out one file, thumbed through it, then placed it back, and opened another drawer. "He is sinning. They have had a lot of success in the US, I've heard, with therapy to change people like him." She pulled out another file, looked through it, placed it under her arm, and left the room.

I stared at my notes from Celestin's interview, then picked up the phone. I called Miriam, the counselor at the NGO where we met refugees. Miriam was a gentle, kind Ugandan woman in her fifties, who I thought might be sympathetic to Celestin, even if she too thought homosexuality was wrong. I asked her if Celestin had ever been subjected to homophobic attacks, even if he didn't identify as gay. Miriam told me that she didn't know of physical attacks, but he was assumed to be homosexual and called names and isolated by other refugees.

After the conversation, I finished writing up Celestin's case. I argued that even if he did not state openly that he was gay, he was perceived as such, and was in danger in Uganda as a result. A moment after I had finished writing, Miriam rang back. "One more thing," she said. "Because of Celestin's –" she hesitated, "mannerisms, his appearance, it hasn't been possible for him to find work. He is relying on assistance from the church, but I am afraid," she paused again, "they will take advantage of him. Do you think you could help?"

I told her I would look into financial assistance for him and let her know.

I approached Patricia and told her about the interview with Celestin and what Miriam had said. She agreed to release financial assistance for Celestin, beginning the following month. I sent the finalized case to our regional office for review. From there, it would be submitted to a resettlement country, to make the final decision about whether to accept him. It could be weeks, months, or even years before he would leave, and it was still possible that no country would take him in, and he would be forced to remain in Uganda.

Soon after the interview with Celestin, I arranged to meet Mario for lunch downtown. We hugged when he arrived, then ordered food: goat stew and rice, and bottles of the local Bell lager to drink. Mario lifted a messenger bag from over his shoulder and pulled out and unfolded a paper. The Red Pepper again. He passed it to me, just as the food arrived.

"Another article." He waited until the server had left, before continuing. "This time about gay women."

I opened the paper, and Mario began eating his stew. The article bore the heading, "Kampala's Lesbians Unearthed," and included a list of names of women who were, again, apparently gay. It read:

To rid our motherland of the deadly vice, we are committed to exposing all the lesbos in the city. Send more names us [sic] the name and occupation of the lesbin [sic] in your neighbourhood, and we shall shame her.

I closed the paper and pulled my knife and fork out from their tightly wrapped napkin. I lifted a forkful of stew to my mouth and ate it slowly. I felt sick. Though the language was preposterous, I knew now that these articles weren't a joke. Since the last article had been published, Mario had told me about men on the list who had lost their jobs, been rejected by their families, or been physically attacked by mobs.

Mario didn't look up from his plate as he ate. I wondered whether his name and photo would be on the next list and whether he would have to leave the country. At least he could go somewhere safe. If Celestin's name appeared on the list, he had nowhere, right now, to go.

The waiter arrived with our bill, and we paid, finished our Bell lagers, and climbed onto the boda-bodas that, seeing us ready to leave, had just pulled up.

Mr & Mrs

Rose placed a file on my desk and stood back. "This is Jackie Nzozi, a Rwandan refugee." She paused, then added, raising her eyebrows, "She's a bit fishy."

I looked from the file to her. "What do you mean?"

Rose shrugged. "There's something dodgy about her story. It doesn't quite ring true. But," she continued, "interview her for resettlement. See what you think."

By now, I had learned just how desperate some refugees were to be resettled to a western country. Since only the most vulnerable refugees were accepted, the worse-off a refugee appeared, or made themselves appear, the greater their chances were of achieving this dream. In order to increase their likelihood of being resettled, then, some refugees fabricated or exaggerated what had happened to them. As a result, we had to check all testimonies carefully. In addition, resettlement countries did their own interviews with clients after we submitted their cases. If we submitted refugees who weren't credible, resettlement countries would become distrustful of our submissions, and they would carry out longer, more in-depth interviews, accepting fewer refugees overall as a result. Refugees who lived in remote camps or settlements, or had urgent, life-threatening illnesses, or were in immediate danger of being killed, were sometimes accepted without a further interview by the resettlement country. These refugees would no longer be accepted at all if our testimonies on their behalf couldn't be trusted.

My colleagues and I had master's degrees and legal and NGO backgrounds, but had no training in lie detection, counseling, or working with people who had experienced severe trauma. We had no formal training in interviewing at all. In an attempt to establish whether a refugee's story was true, we could only check that it didn't change over time or in different family members' accounts, and that it was consistent with externally-available information about events taking place in that area, at that time. Those whose stories we deemed credible were eligible for a new life in the

West; those who we concluded were lying would remain indefinitely in a refugee settlement in Uganda.

People's lives hinged on conclusions that we were unqualified to make.

A week after Rose gave me her file, I arranged to interview Jackie. I met her at the local NGO. Jackie walked slowly, unevenly, with the aid of crutches, to the interview room. She sat down with difficulty. I asked, "What happened to your leg?"

Jackie looked down. "My husband was a soldier with the Rwandan Patriotic Front, and he was killed by men who opposed them. I was shot in the leg at the same time, but managed to escape."

I skimmed through her notes. This was consistent with what she had told my colleagues in earlier interviews. She shifted in her seat and looked around the room. She turned to me, her face fixed in an expression of pain and sadness that seemed fake, insincere. I turned back to her file. A Ugandan doctor's report on her leg was there, but it was inconclusive. He'd stated that her injuries could have been caused by either a car accident or a shooting. There was no indication that anything other than a visual examination had been done: an MRI would have been impossible, and an X-ray prohibitively expensive. The cause of her injuries was critical. A shooting would increase her chances of resettlement – she'd be considered a victim of violence or torture. A car accident would not.

I turned the pages of Jackie's file. "Do you have any living family members?"

She folded her hands on her lap. "My parents and sister were killed in the 1994 genocide. My daughter disappeared in Rwanda."

"Have you tried tracing her?" I asked. "The Red Cross has an office in Kampala – they carry out family tracing."

Jackie looked away. "The office is too far from where I live."

I sighed. It made no sense to me. If I had a child who had disappeared, I would go to any lengths to trace her. I couldn't imagine even leaving the country without her. Not trying to trace her daughter because the office – in the same city – was too far from her house? This made me think that Jackie didn't have a daughter at all.

On occasion, refugees would pay families who were being resettled to pretend that their children were theirs so that they could be resettled with them. They were willing to risk never seeing their child again, in order to give that child a more hopeful future. We were instructed to find children who had been falsely added to a case and to refuse to resettle them or the families who had fraudulently taken them on. For this reason, we often interviewed children separately from their parents, and compared their stories with their parents', to see if they added up. Once, Ali had demanded that a Somali woman living in Brazil fly to Uganda to take a DNA test, to ensure she was really the mother of the child with whom she was asking to be reunited. She borrowed money – risking her life by refusing the lender's demand to transport drugs in return – to fly across the world to prove to us that the boy was hers.

Perhaps Jackie was pretending to have a daughter so that she could, if accepted for resettlement, add another family's child to her case. Still, I had no real evidence to support this theory, or that she was lying about her injuries, so I wrote up her case and submitted it, to be cleared for referral to Canada. I called Jackie to let her know.

Days later, Rose took me aside. "Jackie Nzozi approached me today. She said she had some information for me, but not to share it with you." She shook her head. "I didn't promise that I wouldn't share it, because of course I would."

She took out a page of notes she had made, to be placed in Jackie's file.

"Jackie," she began, "is married. She has been since before she met you, but she didn't want you to know. Her husband, Ahmed, is another refugee." She smirked. "A Somali."

I looked to the page of notes. "Her husband is Somali? A Muslim? But Jackie is a Rwandan Catholic."

Rose's expression was deadpan. "Yes. I smell a rat."

In our experience, it was rare for a Somali to marry a non-Somali; rarer still for a Somali to marry a non-Muslim. The marriage had only been announced when Jackie knew she was going to be resettled. Being married to Jackie meant that this man could be resettled with her. We pondered the possibilities:

The man had given Jackie money to marry him so that he too could be resettled.

The man had otherwise coerced Jackie into marrying him, maybe with violence.

They weren't married at all – only saying so, so that he could be resettled.

I phoned our regional office in Kenya and asked them to put the case on hold. Rose said, "I know what to do."

She pulled open a drawer in her desk, rifled through it, shut it, then opened another. She pulled out empty files, a box of thumbtacks that spilled on her desk, then announced, "Here it is."

She waved two torn sheets of paper, stapled several times together, then pushed them across her desk to me. I stared at the document. It had been typed on a typewriter and photocopied many times over. At the top of the first page was written,

Marriage Verification Questionnaire

What followed appeared to be fifty questions to ask each of the couple – about their marriage and each other – separately, while the other waited in another room. Their answers would then be compared to determine if they really were married.

I should, Rose told me, ask Jackie and Ahmed to meet with me without telling them why, then bring them in one at a time, and ask them the questions. It would be like the old British TV show, *Mr & Mrs.* I had watched the show as a kid, sitting on the brown swirly carpet of our wood-paneled living room in Newry, Northern Ireland.

In the show, couples of all ages would be asked questions about each other:

What color is your husband's toothbrush?
What was the name of your wife's first pet?
What would your husband save in a fire?

The couple who knew each other best took home the prize money. While a contestant was being asked questions about their spouse, the spouse waited in a soundproof cubicle, listening to music on huge headphones and smiling obliviously to reassure the audience that they couldn't hear their partner's answers. I wondered whether we could catch Jackie out using the same techniques.

I asked the filing clerk to bring me Ahmed's file. It told me that he'd fled Somalia after members of his family had been killed in clan-based violence. He was a member of a minority clan in Somalia, which made him vulnerable. There was nothing unusual about his story, no conversion to Christianity, nothing to explain why he would marry a Rwandan Catholic. In the "Languages" section of his biodata, only Somali was mentioned. Jackie barely spoke any English: I communicated with her mainly in French. Her first language was Kinyarwanda, then Swahili, neither of which Ahmed appeared to speak. There was no mention of Jackie or any marriage in Ahmed's file. I placed it inside Jackie's and arranged to meet them both the next day.

The next morning, I went to the area in the front of the NGO where refugees waited for their interviews. Jackie was sitting in the front row of benches, her crutches propped beside her. I called her. The man beside her – Ahmed, I recognized him from the photo in his file – stood up. I waved at him.

"I just need to speak to Jackie first."

He nodded, looking uneasy, and sat down. I stared at him. I hadn't noticed his age in his file, but he appeared to be least ten years younger than Jackie. His expression was even shiftier than hers.

Jackie followed me, walking slowly, to the interview room, and sat down.

I said, "I need to ask you some questions. About your marriage – since you didn't mention it to me before."

She nodded, pulling at a loose thread on the sleeve of her dress. I opened her file and lifted out the Marriage Verification Questionnaire. Though Ahmed was outside with the other refugees, I imagined him wearing huge headphones and grinning at the audience, in a booth next door.

I worked my way through the list of questions. *What did you wear to your wedding? What did your husband eat last night? What is his favorite food? Which of his friends last visited? Does he want to have children? What are his dreams in life?* I could picture the old host of the British gameshow smirking at uncertain answers, winking, cuing the audience to laugh.

Jackie answered almost all of the questions, constantly shifting in her seat, and without making eye contact. When we'd finished, I told her she could leave, but to send Ali in. I called an interpreter to accompany her, so she wouldn't be able to prepare Ahmed. She nodded, silently and looked up at me, an expression almost of defeat. She lifted her crutches, slowly heaved her weight onto them and, with faltering steps, left the room.

I read over her questions when she'd gone. I was looking forward to comparing the answers, to finally catching her out. Then her expression as she left came back to me. What had it said? *Fine, you have all the power. I give up. I can't compete.* I felt a rush of shame. Was I humiliating her? Degrading her? Lording my power over her? I didn't want to acknowledge the possibility. I turned her questionnaire over so the blank back page was facing up.

Ahmed knocked on the door and entered, smiling, his demeanor relaxed in a way that appeared forced. An interpreter appeared behind him, nodded discretely, and sat down. Ahmed thanked me several times as I told him to take a seat. I looked through his file. He was, in fact, thirteen years younger than Jackie. It was impossible: a Somali Muslim who spoke a different language to her, and was much younger?

I lifted the second copy of the Marriage Verification Questionnaire and turned to *Questions for HIM*. There were fifty questions, corresponding to those Jackie had been asked. Ahmed answered them without hesitation, looking bemused. The interpreter fired off his answers. "Last night? I ate matooke. So did my wife."

I checked against Jackie's answer: yes, but everyone in Uganda, it seemed, ate matooke – steamed plantain – every night.

"My wife wore a dress to our wedding."

OK – but what else would she have worn?

"We haven't discussed children."

Correct. I exhausted the fifty questions and re-read both sets of answers. Ahmed hadn't slipped up once. Were the questions too easy, too generic, too vague? But this was, Rose had told me, the standardized questionnaire we always used. It was not possible to add to it or replace it. If a couple gave all the same answers, that was it.

I called Jackie back in, and she took a seat beside Ahmed. They didn't look at each other.

"Jackie," I said, "if you were married when I met you before, why didn't you tell me?"

Jackie began to speak, but Ahmed interjected, "What she meant when she said she wasn't married was – we hadn't consummated our marriage. Because of her injuries. We still haven't, in fact."

I winced. I turned to Jackie. "It would have been better if you'd told me."

She replied without looking at Ahmed or me, and said, "I was afraid to. In case it affected my resettlement application."

I sighed. "How do you even communicate? If you don't speak the same languages?"

Ahmed spoke. "I am learning some Swahili. It's enough that we can understand each other."

I stared at him. "Do you have a marriage certificate?"

Jackie nodded and passed me a copy from her bag. I placed it in her file and told them both they could leave.

Back at the office, I opened Jackie's file and pulled the certificate out. At the bottom was a phone number for the imam at the mosque where they had been married. I called him. He was disgruntled. "If my name is there, it means I married them. It means they're married, yes."

I hung up. They were married. That still didn't say anything about their motives – about whether Jackie had only married this man in order for him to be resettled. A resettlement country reviewing the application would assume it was fraud. The marriage wasn't real, I was still certain, but if it was legal, there was nothing I could do. I opened Ahmed's file and began work on adding him to Jackie's case, so they could be submitted as a couple. If they were accepted together, I wondered, would it encourage more refugees to engage in fake marriages? It felt like such a sham. I finished writing up the argument and submitted it to our regional office to review and forward to a resettlement country.

Jackie and Ahmed's case was submitted for resettlement to Norway. A month later, when we were still waiting for a response, I went to the NGO's office to interview a Congolese family. As I was leaving the office for the afternoon, I glimpsed Jackie and Ahmed in the distance. They were leaving the office too, walking up the hill in the direction of the slums where most of our clients lived. They must have had an appointment for medical assistance since they weren't meeting with me. I looked around for one of our drivers, then caught sight of Jackie and Ahmed again in the corner of my eye and looked back. They had their backs to me. Jackie was holding one crutch, and Ahmed was holding the other, his other arm supporting her. They were laughing as Jackie was stumbling; she was breathless with laughter, and Ahmed was making her laugh more.

I felt the heat rising in my face. What had happened? Had they fallen for each other *after* arranging to marry each other so Ahmed could be resettled? Had they in fact seen me leaving the office and were keeping up their act? But that was impossible. They couldn't have seen me. Had it been a genuine marriage all along?

I looked away. I was beginning to wonder if we were quick to accuse refugees of lying because it let us off the hook. If refugees were lying anyway, what did it matter if our work was sloppy, if we were lazy if we earned thousands of dollars per month while they lived in squalid camps and slums?

But no. A Somali Muslim and a Rwandan Christian: it was impossible.

I looked up again. Ahmed was stroking Jackie's shoulder now as he held it. I had no way to explain it. I sat on the curb, letting my laptop case and files drop beside me. A white UN Landcruiser pulled up a few feet away. The driver, not seeing me, tilted his seat back, put his hands behind his head, and closed his eyes. Jackie and Ahmed were turning the corner now, still laughing. She was holding him, he was helping her walk.

Another Parish

As I finished typing up interviews late on a Monday afternoon, I heard a knock on my office door. There was a slow creak as it was pushed open, then Ali poked his head in. He acknowledged Rose briefly, then smiled at me.

"Could I have a word?"

I nodded and waited, and he frowned, as if to say, *not here*. I turned to Rose, who rolled her eyes, then I stood and followed Ali to his office.

Ali gestured to the chair across from his desk. "Sit down, dear."

He smiled as he took his seat. "Are you free on Thursday night?"

I nodded ambivalently.

"Good!" he exclaimed, then more quietly, "Good. I am having some people over for dinner, and wondered if you would join us."

I exhaled in relief, glad that it wasn't – why would it be? – a one-on-one date. "Yes. Thank you."

He tapped the desk and listed the people he'd invited. Mamadou, a level above Ali and a level below the head of office. Sandrine, also one level below the head of office, but in another department. Patricia, though he rarely acknowledged her, and her husband. Johan, another senior staff member, and his wife. Frieda, the twenty-four-year-old Canadian intern, and her mother, who was in town. Though most of the staff in the office were black, almost everyone on Ali's invite list was white. This, I knew, was why Rose had rolled her eyes when he had wanted to speak to me, but not her. Ali was polite to Rose, but for the most part, she, like the other African staff, was invisible to him. "Make the language easy," he had once told Frieda, preparing a report for him, "so the Ugandans will understand it."

Ali's racism still shocked me, but I found it even more shocking that he had no qualms about expressing it in the context of the UN. I didn't understand why he didn't fear any repercussions for saying these things. Early on, I had wondered, too, why he was doing this work. But this at least, I had learned the answer to. At a meeting with a local NGO, he had boasted – to show his importance perhaps, it wasn't clear – that he earned, with allowances, $200,000 a year. Another senior manager told me that he had left a career in finance to work at the UN as it was, he declared, more lucrative. When I started working, I had no idea of the salaries and benefits of international senior staff. My own "volunteer" stipend had surprised me - $1,700 a month, more than three times what some permanent local staff were earning, and their salary - $500 a month – was already more than ten times what we expected refugees to live on.

I didn't know how to refuse Ali's invitation and feared that he would punish me if I refused to come. Not long before, I had questioned a report he had asked me to write, recommending that it was safe for Rwandan refugees to return, and he had yelled at me, asked me to leave his office, then refused to speak to me for a week. I knew how he reacted if he was challenged or thwarted.

"Thursday at 7pm," he said. "We'll see you there!" Then he sat back and waited for me to leave the room.

On the night of the party, Ali hovered over the Ugandan woman serving the food. She obeyed his instructions nervously, smiling, but not speaking, to any of the guests. Her name was Judith, and she was, Ali said, his full-time housekeeper.

"She's good," he confided, "but you need to teach her. She doesn't know how to do these things on her own."

Judith cleaned Ali's apartment each day while he was at work, and prepared his meals in the evening. I imagined him "teaching" her, giving her exact instructions on how to prepare each dish to his liking, how to polish and scrub the apartment and clean the toilet to his standards.

Frieda, her mother and I had arrived before everyone else. Ali hurried Judith to bring out the wine, and she served it before returning to the food. The other guests streamed in gradually and were greeted effusively by Ali: a hug, followed by a polite request to take off their shoes.

Judith brought the food to us on mother-of-pearl inlaid trays: Middle Eastern hors d' oeuvres she had prepared, she told us, with Ali's guidance. When people finished the contents of their wine glasses, Ali would call for her, and request a prompt refill. The talk was of work, of other colleagues, of the guests' houses in Kampala, and their staff. Judith had prepared fish with lemon and garlic, wrapped it in foil, and set it to cook on the grill on the balcony. We moved outside, some of us congregating around the grill and the cooler of beer Ali had placed beside it.

Late in the evening, when everyone else had moved inside, I found myself alone with Mamadou, the deputy head of the office. Mamadou was Malian but had been educated in Europe. He appeared to be in his forties. He clothes were slick: a white shirt opened two buttons down, loose charcoal-grey pants. He wore black, thick-rimmed glasses: glasses that wouldn't be out of place in a hip bar in New York. His hair was twisted into short, neat dreads. I had spoken to him only once before: the day after I arrived, when he had come to my office with – I never learned why – a basketball, which he bounced from hand to hand on the floor while he talked. "If you ever have any problems," he said – bounce-bounce – "you can come straight to me." His offer had seemed intended, primarily, to undermine Ali, since Ali was my immediate supervisor, and the one I should normally turn to for help.

Now, Mamadou asked how I was getting on in the office, how I was finding the work. I answered him, sipping on the remains of my wine, which had turned warm in the glass. He asked how my living accommodation was, and then, mid-sentence, reached out and touched my breast. He touched it, then let his hand drop to his side again. I stopped drinking suddenly and stared at him. He had turned away, reaching for a piece of fish from the grill. When he turned back, he unwrapped the fish carefully, bunched the foil up in a ball on his plate and then, with a plastic fork, began to eat. He looked up again and resumed the conversation. I thought, *that was a mistake. He reached out to touch – what – my arm? My shoulder? - to make his point, and his hand accidentally grazed my breast.* Yes, it was an accident – there was no other explanation. He hadn't even seemed to notice what he had done. But how was that possible? The alcohol, I concluded, had made him oblivious.

He asked about how I got to the office each day. Did I walk? Take a boda boda? I had finished my drink now, and Judith was passing by again with bottles of cold white wine. I let her refill my glass. Mamadou finished his fish and sat the plate on a plastic patio table behind him. He called Judith back and asked that she refill his glass too. He gestured outwards.

"Nice view."

Ali's apartment was in the hilly neighborhood of Bugolobi, on the outskirts of Kampala, and looked out on a scene of lush, green, banana plantations, and white, colonial-style houses, with terracotta rooftops. I nodded.

"But I think his rent is too high," Mamadou continued.

I looked around. Everyone else was inside.

Suddenly, I felt Mamadou's hand on my breast again and turned back. He let his hand drop and was cradling his wineglass now with both hands. Two times: it couldn't be a mistake. But he had grazed it so lightly. Had he reached out to touch my arm and, drunk, missed it, twice?

"I like this neighborhood," Mamadou continued. "But I still think it's overpriced."

Twice couldn't be a mistake, but how could he have meant to do it either? I could find no way to believe that he would have done it deliberately, would have risked doing it, and so concluded, again, that it was a mistake, though I knew that was unlikely.

I nodded at his comment on the cost of the neighborhood, then excused myself to go to the bathroom and left.

Coming out of the bathroom, I saw Mamadou, inside now, seated on the floor with Frieda and her mother. I looked away quickly and headed towards my colleague Johan, who was standing alone. He pulled a pack of cigarettes from his shirt pocket, flipped open the lid, and offered it to me. I took one and headed out to the balcony again with him to smoke. I stayed there, making small talk – the same topics I'd covered with Mamadou – until it was time to leave.

At ten the next morning, I left the office to smoke a cigarette on the steps outside the conference room. Other smokers congregated there, but now there was no one. A meeting was taking place in the conference room, and it was packed with staff. I sat two steps down, out of their sight. I lit a cigarette, a blue Dunhill – the equivalent of a dollar fifty a pack – and inhaled deeply. The grounds of the office were beautiful – large gardens with tables for eating lunch, shaded by palms, and mango trees. It had rained in the early morning, and the grass was still wet, the air still fresh.

I saw Frieda walk by on her way to the cafeteria and called to her. She looked up and waved, distracted. She continued walking to the cafeteria, then stopped and turned back. She came up the steps and sat one below me, out of the path of the cigarette smoke.

"Did you have a good time last night?" I asked her.

She bit her lip. "That's what I came to talk to you about."

I turned away from her and exhaled smoke into the cool air.

"Did you talk to Mamadou at the party?" she asked.

I turned back suddenly. "Yes. Why?"

Frieda looked away now. "He said some strange things later in the evening. I think you had gone."

I inhaled one last time and stubbed the cigarette out with my foot. The steps were littered with cigarette stubs and burnt-out matches. Once or twice a week, one of the workmen who washed the UN Landcruisers daily and did other odd jobs came and swept them up.

"We were sitting on the floor in Ali's house," Frieda continued. "And he leaned towards my mother, staring at her cleavage, and said, 'You have beautiful breasts.' My mother was horrified. And upset. She couldn't believe that this was where I was working, that this was my boss."

Frieda sighed and looked around. A workman in blue overalls was washing one of the older Landcruisers with a bucket and brush. There was no one else there.

"The thing is," Frieda said quietly, "that wasn't even the first thing that's happened. Mamadou has been harassing me since I arrived."

I pulled another cigarette from the packet and flicked the lighter on. "What do you mean?"

Frieda shook her head. "The day that I arrived, I was sitting in the cafeteria, waiting to meet with Ali. Mamadou approached me. He said, 'I know who you are. You shouldn't be here. You aren't qualified. We all know why Ali picked you from your application.' He looked me up and down – leering. Then he walked off." Frieda shook her head. "I was in disbelief. I had only just arrived! I hadn't done anything to anyone. I had no idea why he was saying this. Then – " she exhaled loudly, "some people invited me to the bar with them that night. I was coming out of the toilets, and Mamadou blocked my exit. He was drunk. He took my hands and said, 'You know why I'm following you. You know how attractive you are. It's not my fault.' I didn't know what to say. He was a senior manager, and I'd just arrived. I was uncomfortable. I thanked him and left soon after."

"That's awful," I said. "I had no idea."

Frieda lifted my cigarette packet, stood it on its side, then sat it down again. "That was only the beginning. A couple of weeks later, Stefan, the security officer, invited me and some others to Jinja for a weekend of white-water rafting. I didn't know that Mamadou was coming too. We were staying in a guesthouse. On the first night, at 4am, I woke to find Mamadou sitting on the side of my bed. He was watching me. I was spooked and asked him to leave. The next morning, I found his shoes still in my room. I returned them to him at breakfast. Stefan saw me give him the shoes and I told him later what had happened. I thought because he was the security officer, he would do something. But he just laughed it off."

I stubbed my second cigarette out and lined the butt up beside the first. I looked out into the parking lot. The workman had finished washing the Landcruiser and had gone. There was no one around. There was a rumor of an office monkey who hung out periodically in the lot and had once stolen a wing mirror from one of the cars. I watched for it, always, as I smoked. I believed in its existence – monkeys were commonplace – and perhaps even in its ability to steal a mirror from a car. Stealing mirrors from cars was so common, however, that I wondered if someone else had done it, and in a moment of inspiration, blamed the monkey.

Frieda sighed. "Since then, Mamadou has called me in the middle of the night about once a week. He asks if he can come see me, and I always politely say 'no.' Last night, he said that although he knew I would be leaving Uganda after my internship, no matter where in the world I went, he would find me."

She looked off towards the cafeteria.

"Have you ever reported him?"

Frieda shrugged. "I did tell Stefan that time. I figured since he was the security officer, he would do something. But he just seemed to find it funny. After that, I didn't see the point. But now – since he upset my mother – he went too far."

I tugged at the foil of the cigarette pack and pulled it out. I rolled it into a tiny cylinder between my thumb and forefinger. In the conference room, I could see people yawning, while someone I didn't know scribbled numbers and diagrams on a flip-chart.

I didn't understand why Frieda hadn't tried harder to report what Mamadou had done. The deputy head of office had crept into her bedroom, and sat on her bed, watching her sleep. He'd called her in the middle of the night, and stalked her.

It was clear now that his touching my breast the night before was not a mistake. I was furious, ready to report that now, to see him disgraced and fired.

"Last night," I told Frieda, "Mamadou was talking to me, and he reached out and touched my breast. Just like that, in the middle of conversation. I was sure it was accidental. Then he did it again, but again I concluded it was an accident, though I didn't understand how it could be. After that, I left."

Frieda's eyes widened. "He did it to you too?"

I nodded. "We need to report him."

Frieda looked away. She was silent for a long time, then said, eventually, "I'm only an intern here. I need references to find work. Let me think about it first."

Just before lunch, there was a knock on my office door. Claudia, the twenty-one-year-old British intern, pushed the door open timidly and asked if she could come in.

She sat down, and said finally, "Can I ask you something?"

I nodded. She had never approached me like this before.

"Last night, were you at Ali's house? Was Mamadou there?"

I pushed aside the file I had been reading and turned my chair around to face hers.

"Yes. Why?"

She looked away. She had begun to cry.

"What happened?"

Claudia pressed the heels of her hands to her eyes. I'm too embarrassed to say it, so I've written it down." She leaned across the desk and passed me a frayed piece of paper, torn from a spiral-bound notebook. On it was written, in tiny, timid, blue handwriting:

I was at the Irish bar with some other interns last night. At about 11pm, Mamadou and Johan arrived. Mamadou was drunk. He sat beside me, and Johan sat across from us. Mamadou told me I was beautiful and tried to kiss me. I pulled away. Then he told Johan that the reason I wouldn't be with him was because I was a man. He groped my crotch and said, "Look, she has a penis! I told you she was a man." Johan just laughed. Then Mamadou grabbed my breasts and felt them, and said to Johan, "Even these aren't real." Johan laughed again. Then Mamadou said to Johan, "And did you know she's British? You know how you can tell? By the smell of her pussy! Can't you smell it from there?"

When I looked up, Claudia was crying. "I'm so sorry," she said. "I was too embarrassed to tell you – that's why I wrote it down."

I nodded and passed the paper back to her. She stared at it and tore off the frays from the spiral bind, neatly, one by one.

"Some other things happened with Mamadou last night," I told her. "You aren't alone." I picked up the phone. "Frieda can tell you. I'm going to call her to come here."

Frieda came to my office straight away. I passed her Claudia's note. She read it, grim-faced.

I said, "I'm going to report him."

Frieda paused, then nodded. Claudia, taking the paper back, folding it slowly into a small square in her hands, did too.

I called Patricia and said we had to report some incidents of sexual harassment with Mamadou. She told us we needed to speak to the head of office, Linda, and she would arrange an appointment. Ten minutes later, she called back to tell us that Linda would meet with us at her apartment, close to the office, the next morning, which was Saturday.

That afternoon, waiting for a car to come to bring us back to the office following a meeting with another UN agency, I told Ali what had happened. He turned pale. "Do not," he said, "tell anyone that you have told me this. No one must know that I know. I want to be left out of this completely."

Linda, the head of office, was Canadian, a white woman with strawberry blonde hair who was, perhaps, in her early sixties. The local staff worshipped her or pretended to. She was stout, maternal-looking, and wore peach-colored linen suits. She was a lawyer by training. Her husband was a lawyer too but had given up his career to follow her wherever she was posted. I had had no encounters with her, had only seen her at meetings, or occasionally in the cafeteria.

Waking on Saturday morning, I steeled myself for the meeting with her. She would be outraged. Mamadou would be gone after this; other staff would learn of the reason for his departure, and a message would be sent.

Frieda, Claudia, and I walked to Linda's apartment, following directions from Patricia. In front of the apartment block, one of Claudia's plastic flip-flops caught in some gravel, and she fell. Her knee was cut wide open like a child's. She stumbled, trying to stand up. Her eyes were filled with tears. She said, "I'm so embarrassed."

We helped her walk and made our way up the stairs to Linda's apartment, which was on the top floor.

Linda caught sight of Claudia's bleeding knee as soon as we walked in. She told us to sit down and called to her husband to bring a warm soapy cloth and band-aid.

Linda was dressed in her home clothes: a loose blouse, slacks, and pale pink fluffy slippers. Her apartment was huge and stuffed with African artifacts: wooden sculptures, paintings, tribal masks.

When Claudia had finished cleaning and bandaging her knee, Linda asked if her husband could bring us tea. We declined, too nervous to accept. She sat back and asked us what had happened.

Claudia had written everything down this time; she didn't wish to speak at all. Linda took her testimony and read it over, then put it aside. Frieda described what had happened to her at Ali's house, and in the weeks before. I told her about the incident with Mamadou touching my breasts. She nodded, expressionless, throughout. Finally, she stood and said, "Come to my office at nine on Monday morning. I need to look up our policies and procedures for all of this. I can get back to you then."

I got up, surprised that she hadn't said anything else; hadn't expressed any shock. Perhaps, I reasoned, she had to appear neutral, removed, until there was more proof that what we said was true.

Two days later, Claudia, Frieda, and I entered Linda's office. The room was huge, with a heavy oak desk at one end, and leather sofas and a glass coffee table at the other. Oil paintings by local artists decorated the wall. The room was one of the few in the building that was air conditioned, but fans stood by Linda's desk and the sofas, just in case. We waited for her cue, then sat, the three of us together, on one of the leather sofas. Linda sat on the facing sofa. She placed a file of documents on the coffee table in front of her and put on her glasses, which hung from a gold-colored chain around her neck. She looked up at us.

"I consulted these documents on our sexual harassment policy over the weekend. Here are your choices on how to proceed." She looked from one of us to the other, unsmiling, and continued. "I can arrange for a third party to mediate, so you can meet with Mamadou and talk about what happened. This person would function as a sort of counselor. She will help you talk about the events with him so that you can all move on. Or," Linda opened the file in front of her, then shut it again, "I can call the Inspector General's Office in Geneva." She paused, her expression grim. "The Inspector General's representative would have to fly here from Geneva. They would interview almost everyone in the office. Everyone would know everything." Linda paused again, her gaze fixed on Claudia, who was pale. "The investigation would take months," she continued. "At the end, a report would be produced. The representatives would have to come here to conduct interviews several times."

Claudia spoke to Linda. Her expression was one of terror. "I don't think," she began quietly, "that's necessary." She turned to me, then to Frieda. "I don't think we need to fly someone from Geneva and interview everyone in the office and tell them everything that has happened. Do you?"

Frieda shook her head. I said nothing.

Linda nodded. "The third option is that I speak to Mamadou, and convey that these last events have come to my attention, and must never happen again." She folded her arms and sat back.

Claudia looked to each of us anxiously. "For my part, the last option." Then to Frieda and me, "Don't you think?"

Frieda played with the folds of her skirt. "I guess that would be best."

I looked to both of them, then to Linda. "Do we have to decide now? Can we discuss and get back to you?"

Linda smiled tightly. "If you want."

I turned to Frieda, and she said, "Sure."

Claudia nodded reluctantly and bit her lip.

I didn't understand. Why was Linda discouraging an investigation? I felt sick in the pit of my stomach. Was this it? But Frieda and Claudia were intimidated now by Linda's description of how the investigation would unfold. Surely later, reflecting on what had happened, they would change their minds?

In my office that afternoon, I received an email from Frieda. She began, *Ali has invited me to dinner! Emin Pasha – yum! We're going on Friday night. I wonder why he's invited me?*

I sat back and stared at the screen. Emin Pasha was known for being one of the best, and certainly most expensive, restaurants in Kampala. Why was Ali bringing his intern there? And was he bringing her there alone?

"Good luck," I wrote back, and nothing else.

On the Monday after Frieda's dinner with Ali, over a week after our meeting with Linda, Frieda sent me another email.

Ali said some things at dinner, she wrote, *that made me realize that we should probably just leave things with Mamadou. Let Linda talk to him, that's all. Are you OK with that?*

I replied, *What happened?*

An hour passed, then another email from Frieda.

You know I'm only an intern here. I have so much debt from my MA. When I graduate next year, I really need to be able to find work.

I wrote back again. *What did he say?*

Another hour passed, then another reply.

He said that if I reported Mamadou, everyone in Geneva would know. He said my name would be mud. I'd never work for the UN again. It's just – I can't afford to rule out that work. I have $30,000 of debt, and that's before I even start my last year. I think we should ask Linda to speak to Mamadou, as she said she would. She said she would ensure it would never happen again. That's the important thing, isn't it? I think we should just leave it at that.

I stared at her email. If Frieda and Claudia didn't want to call in the inspectors and be subjected to interview, I couldn't force that upon them. I couldn't subject Claudia to more trauma if this is how it would impact her. She and Frieda had been more affected by Mamadou's actions than I had: the choice about what action to take was theirs.

But why had Linda and Ali discouraged them – warned them against – reporting? Because an investigation might uncover misconduct of theirs too? I sat back. In that moment, I could see how everything worked, how managers like Mamadou and Ali could hold their posts – be promoted even, how junior staff could be treated this way, and stay quiet. But still, not here – not in a humanitarian organization, not in an organization dedicated to helping some of the most vulnerable people on earth? Or yes. The evidence had mounted against me, finally. This was how it worked. Here.

I read Frieda's email again, then wrote back, *Fine*.

At lunch in the cafeteria, Frieda sat across from me, and when everyone at our table had left, leaned forward, and whispered. "Ali said something else when he took me out to dinner Friday night." She looked around and, confident that no one at the other tables was within hearing distance, continued. "He said that the only reason Mamadou was in the position he's in was because *they needed a black face in management*."

Mamadou did not show up at the office the next day, or the day after that. We learned, eventually, that he was out "on sick leave." We learned too that Linda had spoken to him. She told us that he "was very sorry" about what had happened, and it wouldn't happen again. We didn't hear from him directly and didn't see him after that.

Mamadou continued to be off work until we learned that he wouldn't, in fact, ever be coming back. He had been transferred to head office in Geneva. It was later that we learned that this transfer, in fact, involved a promotion. "It's like," a friend who worked for another organization told me, "you work for the Catholic Church. A senior figure is involved in sexual harassment, so they *transfer him to another parish*."

Discussing Mamadou's move over lunch in the cafeteria, Claudia expressed her relief.

"That's all I wanted – not to have to see him again."

Frieda agreed. "The important thing was that he wouldn't do it again, and now that Linda has spoken to him, I'm sure that he won't. And at least he's out of our lives."

I thought of the church scandals in Ireland, the abuse by priests, the cover-ups. Had those at the receiving end of that thought the same thing: *not in this organization, surely?* How long had it taken them to believe that this was really happening? Before, I had thought: why didn't' they *just speak up?* Why didn't *I* now?

I thought about Mamadou. He had been working at the UN for many years, would have been promoted many times to reach the position he had now. He had behaved like this with at least three staff in less than two months. I wondered how many other staff he had treated similarly, and how, after so many years, he had come to be certain that he could behave this way with impunity. This was Claudia's first humanitarian post: her first job of any kind. *This* was what she being led to expect?

Mamadou was one of the highest-level staff in an office charged with protecting refugees, pretty much the most vulnerable people in the world. He didn't work directly with refugees now, but he would have, once. I wondered whether he had ever sexually harassed any. There were rumors, always, of staff in other offices, other countries, who had demanded sex from refugees in order to resettle them. It was possible: many refugees, in desperation, could, I was sure, agree to this for a chance at a new life. Still, I had never quite believed it could actually happen, or not here.

I had heard too that the previous High Commissioner – the person appointed by the UN to oversee the protection of refugees worldwide – had been forced to resign just the year before, following accusations of sexual harassment. Various female staff alleged that he had groped them. One said that he had made unwelcome advances and asked her to come to his hotel because he was feeling lonely. The story had seemed so unlikely when I'd first heard it. Now, I wondered if the story of Mamadou would sound the same way if we told others about it: exaggerated, impossible to believe.

An official investigation found that the allegations against the High Commissioner were substantiated and that he had abused his authority in his attempts to influence the investigation's outcome. The findings of the investigation were kept hidden by the UN, and the High Commissioner remained in place, until, the following year, the report was exposed by a newspaper in the UK. It was only after this that he resigned. At a farewell meeting, he was awarded the first annual UNHCR Achievement Award for exceptional services to the organization and the world's refugees.

If the High Commissioner – the person charged by the UN with overseeing protection of refugees worldwide – sexually harassed his staff, and was rewarded with an achievement award in return, there was no reason for Mamadou, or any other staff member, not to believe that they could get away with harassing female staff too. And if Linda wanted to cover up ongoing harassment in the office, she would reward those managers who supported her. Corrupt staff promoted corrupt staff. The local staff, on low salaries with few opportunities for other work – could not speak up, and their inability to protest allowed the corruption to continue. It was supported from both above and below.

I looked at Frieda and Claudia, sipping Fanta, not talking, eating scoopfuls of rice in peanut sauce. At another table, Ali sat, smoking. He flicked through the Daily Monitor, a local paper, then raised his hand to command the cafeteria woman's attention: "A cup of Nescafé, and please remember" – he looked pained, as though he resented having to explain this yet again – "only one sugar."

Every Drop Counts

After leaving the Indians' place, I moved to a one-bedroom house that overlooked downtown Kampala and, in the distance, Lake Victoria, glittering blue and bordered by tall palms. It was one of fifty identical cinder-block houses staggered over a hill in Kololo, the greenest, airiest part of the city. They had been built, in better times, for the staff of the Ugandan electricity board. Now the residents were staff from international businesses and aid organizations. Many worked for the UN – for UNHCR, or the World Food Program, or Unicef, the Children's Fund. Mario's house was just a couple of blocks down from mine.

Guards for the houses sat around on grassy slopes, eating avocados they had pulled from the trees, or listening to football on a tiny battery-operated radio, cheering or crying out in dismay. At the bottom of the hill was a sprawling slum, where local families lived in huddled shacks. There was no running water in the slum other than one rusty communal tap. The children ran in oversized flip-flops, skirting the watery red mud that trickled down the hill in the gutter.

Every month for several months, a water bill arrived at my house, but I didn't pay. Each time a bill came, I resolved to pay it, before stuffing it into a drawer or accidentally throwing it out. On a day at the end of the rainy season, a new letter came. I sat on a cushioned chair on my terrace and tore the envelope open. It read:

National Water and Sewerage Corporation
WATER IS LIFE AND EVERY DROP COUNTS
Dear esteemed customer,

As our valued customer, we wish to extend our sincere appreciation for your efforts at paying your bills. However, our records clearly show that your account has unpaid arrears of .../= which you should settle without further delay.

You are therefore requested to clear your current bill and arrears within two (2) days from the date of delivery of this letter.

Please take immediate action to avoid disconnection of supply.

'THE CUSTOMER IS THE REASON WE EXIST'

The figure for the arrears hadn't been filled in, and I had no idea how much money I owed. I sat back and stared at the lake, which was still shimmering as the sun went down. The lake was the source of the White Nile, and a dam near the head of the river provided most of the country's electricity. I had heard that the water level was falling – because of reduced rainfall or increased demand, or perhaps both – and electricity, in the houses that had it, was rationed to alternate days as a result. I looked back at the letter and thought: *they wouldn't really disconnect my water supply.* Even if, their sincere appreciation notwithstanding, I hadn't made any efforts at paying my bills. But I told myself, this time, I would pay.

For the next two days, the letter didn't come into my head. On the third day, I was late leaving for work. My boda driver was waiting outside. I waved to him and smiled apologetically. He shook his head to tell me it was fine. As I gathered my bag and my coffee, I remembered the letter. I grabbed it and what old bills I could find and shoved them into my purse.

In the evening, after work, I stood outside the gate of our office, waiting to hail a boda. A Congolese refugee was sitting by the gate, breastfeeding her baby. The police who guarded the office told her to leave, but she pleaded with them and eventually they left her alone. She gestured to me. "Madame. Please. I cannot stay here. I have been here for five years already. I don't want to live. All my friends have been resettled – to America, Australia. Why not me? I have no money to eat, it's too hard to feed my baby." She gestured to the tiny child wrapped in a kanga – a sheet of patterned fabric with a message in Swahili – in her arms. "Why have you forgotten about me?"

I looked around. The guards were watching through the bars of the gate. I spoke to her, my voice low. "I can't help you here. You have to make an appointment and go to the NGO's offices for an interview."

"Madame," the woman pleaded. "Madame. You know how many times I have been there, and no assistance. Still, I am here. I have nothing, no one helps me, five years I am here, and I have to beg for money, my two children can't go to school, we live in one dirty room with nothing in it, no water, no power, we sleep, five of us on the ground, my baby has no food."

I nodded, looking around. The guards were watching us with disdain. "I know. I'm sorry. But I can't do anything here. You have to go to the other office – go early tomorrow morning. Tell the staff everything. They will see if you are eligible for resettlement."

The woman's eyes had welled up now. A tear fell slowly down her cheek. The baby, unsettled, began to cry, and she coaxed him back to her breast.

"Madame. The staff there – they will tell me to go away. They will say they have heard my story before, and now I have to wait. But how long? How long do I have to live like this?"

I stared at the baby. The kanga was thin and knotted loosely around him. "I don't know. I'm sorry. There are procedures. Everyone who is resettled has to be interviewed at the NGO's office first. We have –" I paused. "We have a lot of refugees. Two hundred and forty thousand people. Every year, only eight hundred or so are resettled. That's how it is."

She raised her eyebrows. "Eight hundred? Why only eight hundred?"

"That's how many we have the capacity to do." I felt a stabbing in my chest as I said this. We could probably work harder and do more, but surely then we'd burn out? No, I tried to tell myself, this was as much as we could do, as many people as we could help.

The woman said, "Madame, you are the one who can help me. Please don't forget."

A boda driver pulled up and waved. I nodded at him and turned back toward the woman. "The NGO, tomorrow morning. They might be able to help you." She looked away. As the motorbike pulled off, I could see that the baby was crying again, and the kanga had come undone, exposing his belly and tiny genitals.

The boda brought me to the offices of the National Water and Sewerage Corporation, where I joined a queue that stretched almost to the door. Everyone ahead of me stood in silence, still, upright. Two of the women had babies tied to their backs, sleeping, their mouths open. A man at the front turned around to stare at me, looked up and down at my pale skin, then turned back, his bill clasped in his hand. When I reached the front, I handed the teller my letter. She looked at it and gave me a form. It was to confirm that I was paying my bill. I asked her for a pen. She looked irritated, then passed me her biro. When I'd filled out the form and given it back, she read it and looked perturbed, as though she hadn't realized what it was for. She brought it to her colleague in the next booth. They discussed it in Luganda, and then she returned.

"Madam," she said sorrowfully, "the machine it is – what? – not working. Now we are – what? – not processing bills."

I looked around. "Can I leave the money for the bill and you can process it when the machine is fixed?"

The teller left again to consult with her colleague. She returned to tell me that I could. The teller and her colleague made me a handwritten receipt and told me the money would go into the account as soon as the machine was functioning again. I left with the receipt and hailed a boda for home.

Two days later, Mario stopped by. The inside of Mario's house was the same as mine, but the built-in shelves, instead of holding biographies of African leaders and books on rethinking aid, were lined with pornographic magazines and DVDs, smuggled in from Europe.

Mario asked if I had water in my house and I told him that I did. All the houses on the hill shared the same water mains. Sometimes it was switched off, and we relied on the water in our tanks until it was switched back on. Now, Mario said, the water had been off for so long that his tank had run out. I checked my tap: I still had water. Mario shrugged. "Maybe my maid used it up, washing clothes."

That night, I received a text message from my landlord. It read, *Yr water is off right now. U will need to economize.*

The next morning I went to see my neighbor Gloria, a Tanzanian woman who worked for UNDP, and she told me she'd run out of water too. She and the woman who lived next to her were going to a hotel after work to shower. My own tank was still not empty. For a moment I worried that I must be washing less than everybody else.

The next day, Saturday, Mario stopped by to tell me that now he was refilling his toilet cistern with Coca-Cola. He sat on the porch, and I went inside to make coffee. I turned the tap in the kitchen, and it spluttered and dribbled into the basin of the sink. After a few seconds, the dribble petered out. I went out to the porch and told Mario I was finally out of water. He smirked, leaning back and stretching his arms behind his head, then sat up suddenly. "Ugh. I need to wash." He stood up. "I'm going to shower at my friend Charles's house. Do you want to come?"

I shook my head. "I'll buy bottled water from the market."

Mario looked off at the lake in the distance. "The water has been off at the mains for three days now. What can possibly be causing it?" He sighed, tugged at his shirt-sleeves where they'd wrinkled from stretching, and left.

I sat down on the porch and watched the wind stir the leaves of the palms at the edge of the lake. If the water company wanted to switch off the water supply to my house, it would have had to switch off the mains serving the entire hill. My stomach began to turn in panic. Was that what had happened? I tried to calculate. I'd paid my bill three days after it had arrived, not two as the letter had stipulated. Maybe the tellers had forgotten about it, or their machine was still broken, and the money hadn't yet been lodged.

The water at the mains had been switched off four days after I'd received the bill. It had never been off for more than half a day before this, never long enough for our tanks to run dry.

I walked to the main road and hailed a boda driver. I asked him to bring me to Kisementi, a noisy square of stalls and traders at the bottom of the hill. As we pulled up at the boda stand, I asked my driver to wait while I went to the supermarket to buy water. He smiled and said, "Of course! I will be here for you, madam. Don't forget me!" and leaned back on the motorbike, chewing on a toothpick in the corner of his mouth.

I made my way to the supermarket on the other side of the square. Men hawked electronic mosquito zappers and 3-D Jesus pictures, bed-sheets and towels stacked high on their heads. The DVD men waved pirated DVDs at me – *Black American Favorites, War Movies Africa, The Terrorism Movies: Part I*, all with badly photocopied covers. I shook my head, smiling. The banana boys, who were between about ten and fourteen years old, carried baskets of stumpy sweet bananas and pineapples on their heads. They ran towards me as I approached, calling "Madam, bananas! Last time you promised!" It was true – the last time I had escaped them by promising "next time." But I still didn't want any bananas, and I smiled apologetically and walked past them quickly into the supermarket.

I bought fifteen three-liter bottles of water. The packer tied them up in plastic bags and carried them to the boda for me. The boda driver hooked half of the bags over his handlebars and passed the others to me to hold between my knees. We pulled off unsteadily, then he gained speed, and I clutched his jacket as he sped up the hill. We passed women walking slowly with enormous bundles of firewood on their heads, and they stared at me, a white woman on the back of a boda with forty-five liters of water.

At home, I washed myself in a plastic basin then poured the washed-in water into the cistern of the toilet; when I flushed it, the soap-suds bubbled furiously in the bowl. Each flush used seven three-liter bottles, and soon, there was no water left. I hailed a boda from the top of the hill and asked the driver to bring me again to Kisementi. This time in the square, there were other white people – mzungus – from the houses on the hill, and men and women from the slum below. People were sitting on the pavement selling yellow jerry cans of water. They must have transported them by boda from another part of town. The mzungus were queuing to buy them; the supermarket, I was told, had sold out of bottled water completely. I walked back to the boda. A woman who worked as a maid for one of my neighbors was setting off up the hill carrying a jerry can on her head. Her seven-year-old son walked beside her, his hand against the jerry can on his head to stop it from falling. A guard from the hill balanced one on his head and carried another in each hand. I joined the queue of mzungus and bought two full jerry cans. As I walked to the boda rank past the people with jerry cans on their heads and tied to bicycles, I thought, *You are all here because of me. I can never tell anyone this is my fault.*

Soon after I returned home, Mario appeared again on the porch. He kissed me on each cheek, then said excitedly, "So I've been invited to this party. Some Spanish people, on the other side of town. Wanna come? They have water! We can use their toilet, and, if you want, I'm sure they'll let us wash."

I thought about this. If I didn't go, I wouldn't have washed properly in three days. "Sure," I said.

Mario nodded cheerfully. "That's great. Nine o'clock? Want to drink gin on my terrace before we go? Come to my house first, and I'll make gin and tonics."

I plucked a dead leaf from a plant outside my house. "Mario, what do you think has caused the water mains to be switched off for so long?"

"I have no idea," Mario replied nonchalantly. "But I wonder when it will come back on. Or if it will ever come back. Maybe this is it?" He laughed. "I spread my laundry on the grass in front of my house in case it rains. And left out all my rubbish bins too to catch the water." He looked out at my garden. "You should do the same. It could rain tonight."

He left, kissing me again and reminding me to come by later for gin. I watched him walk back to his house and thought, *There is no point in telling anyone now. There's nothing I can do. I've paid the bill, so I just have to wait for them to process it and turn the water back on.* I sat on the bamboo chair. *But what if there's an outbreak of cholera? People are going to die because I'm a loser who never gets around to paying her bills.*

I went inside and called Gloria to see if she knew anything more. She told me she'd complained to the landlord. He said he'd tried to call the water board to see what the problem was, but couldn't get through. I began to feel nauseous. I paced from the living-room to the bedroom and back. I was disgusting, I stank, and thousands could die because I was lazy and careless and inconsiderate.

I went into the bathroom. I could flush the toilet or wash, not both, and I couldn't go to the party smelling this bad, so I poured one jerry can into the bath. It was cold and filled only a couple of centimeters. I squeezed in the end of a bottle of South African bath foam I had bought at the only shopping mall in the city. I undressed, let my clothes drop onto the floor, and squatted in the shallow cold water, using a sponge to squeeze water down my back and scooping up foam with my hand. The water made me shiver. I poured the rest of it over my head slowly, rinsing my shampoo out. When I'd finished, I stepped out of the tub, trembling with cold, and pulled a towel from the rail. I picked out a dress from the wardrobe, where my maid had hung it up, crease-less from rigorous ironing. I dressed and sprayed eucalyptus oil on my wrists and ankles to ward off mosquitoes, then headed to Mario's house.

Mario was already sitting on his terrace, a glass of gin and tonic in his left hand, a book I'd lent him in his right. He stood and embraced me, smiling widely, still holding the glass of gin. Without asking, he poured some gin into a glass for me, flicked open a can of tonic water, and squeezed a tiny, bumpy, dark green lime. We sat on low fat-cushioned seats and looked out to the lights flickering on around the lake.

"You know," Mario told me, "I have a problem here."

I sat my glass on the ground and waited for him to continue.

"Ugandan men," he said, "are almost always bottoms. Rarely tops."

I stared at him. "What do you mean?"

He gestured with his glass. "They like to take, not give."

I raised an eyebrow to indicate I still didn't understand.

"You know – they don't want to penetrate, just to be penetrated."

I lifted my glass from the ground and sucked in a mouthful. "That's not … what you want?"

He shrugged. "I want both! I want them to do it to me. It's funny – almost every Ugandan is the same." He sat back in contemplation.

I tried to push out the images he had planted in my mind. I didn't even know how anyone could be brave enough to be openly gay in Uganda.

After almost an hour, Mario looked to his watch and sat his glass down. "I suppose we should go." He stood up, then leaned down and peered at me. "Did you wash?"

I nodded. "Sort of. With two jerry cans of cold water."

He stood back and exclaimed, "You cheated!"

I laughed, now a little drunk. "What do you mean? I washed for the party! I was disgusting before. You saw me – you know it's true."

"Honey," Mario carried on, "I had sex with two different men yesterday, and I still haven't washed. We were supposed to be dirty together."

I snorted. Mario stretched out his arms and laughed. "But I guess we can still be dirty together, right?"

I sat with my arms around Mario's belly on the back of a boda, downhill all the way to the party.

"I would have brought my car," Mario shouted to me, his hair flying back in the wind, "but I had my right wing-mirror stolen, and I drove to a shop to buy a new one, parked, and when I came out with the new right wing-mirror, the left one had been stolen!" He laughed riotously, throwing his head back. I laughed to the point where I became unbalanced and had to grab onto his shirt.

"Did you have to take a driving test here?"

He guffawed. "A test? I failed my test six times in Europe. Six times! They told me I'd never be able to drive. Here, they saw I was a mzungu, I paid one hundred dollars, and they presented me with a license. You're a mzungu here, you can do anything."

The driver turned his head at the word *mzungu*, looking bemused.

"Dude, look at the road!" I screamed, and all three of us laughed as he swerved to avoid another boda.

"It's true," I told Mario. "I was at a crafts market once, and a woman asked me to look after her stall while she went off to find change. I know she would never have done that with another Ugandan. Because I'm a mzungu, there's no way I'd steal?"

Mario nodded, his hair still blowing back. "Absolutely, that's what she was thinking. And because I'm a mzungu, it's impossible for the license people to believe I wouldn't be able to drive! Ha! They've never seen me behind a wheel. I had two almost-accidents just driving the car home after I bought it."

Giggling, I buried my head into his shoulder. My hair, still not quite clean, was frizzy from the humid air.

The last stretch of road was potholed from the rains, but our driver negotiated the craters undaunted. The shudder of music led us to the house we were looking for. A huge and gnarled mango tree stood in front of the gate. Two guards on stools by the tree watched us arrive, expressionless. Another guard stood in a tiny sentinel hut behind the gate, looking out. As we climbed off the boda, the driver asked for one thousand shillings more than the price we had agreed on. Mario scoffed. The driver pleaded, "But sir, it is further than you told me. And you," he looked from Mario to me, "are two. Please sir, it is more than you said."

Mario turned to walk off. "Two thousand shillings – we agreed!" He turned to me: "Come on."

I shrugged, smoothed my hair into place, and gave the driver five hundred shillings more. He looked disappointed but said, "Thank you, madam," before revving off. The guard in the hut looked us up and down, unlocked the gate, and pulled it open for us, not speaking.

The patio and garden in front of the house were thronged with people sitting on bamboo sofas and hand-carved wooden armchairs, and lying on kangas spread on the grass amongst fallen, overripe avocados. They sipped from bottles of Tusker beer dripping with condensation and glasses of gin mixed with lemon Krest. Music was pounding from giant speakers tied to the trunks of palms. Mario whispered to me, "I'm going to use the toilet all night, just because I can."

"Me too," I laughed.

Mario looked around. "I'm going to find the Spaniards, ask if I can shower first." He threw back his shoulders. "You never know who you might meet. I don't want to score in this condition – smelling of day-old sperm. Times two." He cackled, and I shook my head, feigning disbelief. Mario walked off to find the house's owners, and I made my way to the makeshift bar.

The coolers were stuffed with ice, and I thought about stealing it. There was enough that if I poured it into plastic bags and let it melt, I might be able to wash again the next day. I looked around. How could I explain what I was doing? I'd have to wait until the end of the night when everyone had gone home. I pulled out a bottle of beer and flipped off the lid with a giraffe-shaped opener tied with string to the cooler. Someone tickled my neck from behind, and I jumped. It was Kate, an English friend who worked for a development NGO. I hadn't seen her for weeks: she had been on R & R and travelled to Ethiopia. We embraced. She wore a blue and white cotton scarf draped across her shoulders. Her face and arms were newly tanned. "Long time!" she exclaimed, and I responded with, "You've been lost!" echoing her mock-Ugandan English. She led me across to the corner of the patio where her colleagues were seated. Leaning against the patio railings, she told me about her trip to Ethiopia, the food she had tasted, and the paintings and clothes she had bought. "This is from Addis" – she gestured to the scarf. I nodded in appreciation.

We downed our drinks and opened more from the cooler. Others joined us, white NGO and UN workers drinking African beer, and Ugandans drinking sugary dark orange Fanta and warm Coke. The music had been turned up louder, and a group of Ugandans were dancing in the middle of the garden. I caught sight of Mario, freshly washed, his hair glistening with lavish quantities of styling product, talking to another man by the wall beside the gate. He was laughing, his head tilted coquettishly. The other man appeared to be Ugandan and was shyer, smiling, his expression coy. He was wearing a sleeveless shirt that was a little torn around the neck. His biceps were astonishing – huge, shining as though oiled, with bulging veins. I watched Mario talk to him, but he didn't notice me.

On the bar-table, there were tall bottles of Rwenzori-brand water, and I spent the rest of the night drinking as much as I could. Eventually, Mario having disappeared, I piled into a car with Kate and a couple of her colleagues. David, their driver, asked, "Home?" and Kate's friend in the front seat, laughed and said, "No, ssebo, to the Irish bar. Then drop Karen at her house."

There were crowds in front of the Irish bar, large groups of mzungus and some Ugandans, young Ugandan women holding hands with older mzungu men. Kate and her friends climbed out of the car, and Kate leaned back in to kiss me goodbye. "You're sure you don't want to join us?"

I shook my head and smiled. If I drank any more, I'd need to pee all night, but be unable to flush the toilet.

Kate made her way into the crowd. David turned the key in the ignition and looked back to me. "Where exactly in Kololo, madam?" I gave him directions and sat back. As we ascended the hill, we passed the occasional lone man, a package wrapped in a kanga in his hand or on his head.

The guards at the gate of the compound eyed David with suspicion. I pulled the back window down and leaned out. Upon seeing me, they cried, "Ah, sorry, madam, we are not seeing you – you are welcome," and dragged open the iron gates to let us through.

David waved my thanks away with "Yes, madam. Goodnight."

I walked down the steps to my house, the guards watching me dutifully, then waving as I unlocked the door and stepped safely inside.

I peed before going to bed and, unable to flush, pushed the toilet lid down. The only drink I had left in the house was a bottle of flat tonic water, which I poured into a glass. I lay back on my bed, untied the mosquito net and pulled it carelessly down. Hazy with alcohol, I lay awake for a while, half-dreaming, kicking the sheets down, too hot, before finally falling asleep.

In the middle of the night, I woke up. Water was spluttering and gushing loudly into the tank in the alcove above the bedroom door. The supply was back. I turned over, happy, and went back to sleep.

The following afternoon I edged out of bed, shielding my eyes with my hand, and made my way to the bathroom. I used the toilet and flushed it. I ran the bath, letting it fill almost to the top, got in and lay back. The guards were chattering somewhere outside. After half an hour, Mario called. Dripping, I pulled a towel around me and lifted the phone. Mario was exultant. "It's back! It came back! I flushed the toilet five times this morning, just because I could. This water is giving me so much pleasure!"

I laughed, pulling the towel tighter as a guard walked past the window. The water in the bath would get cold while I spoke, but I could always fill it again. "The landlord," Mario told me, "said a pipe on the road below the compound burst, so they switched the water off until it was fixed."

I didn't respond. I was afraid the guard would walk past again and sat low on the sofa to be out of his view. He was the same guard I had seen carrying the jerry cans of water up the hill on his head and in his hands. I pulled the towel closer around me and stared out at the lake. The water had been off for four days in all. The people who couldn't pay for bottled water would have struggled to wash or cook or drink for that time. But then, most people didn't have running water at all. For a moment I felt relieved, thinking that at least it wasn't my fault.

My Sister

Ayaan was a Somali refugee who lived alone with her seven children in a squalid Kampala slum. She came to meet me at the NGO, holding a sleeping baby against her chest. She ushered her other children around the desk, to make room to close the door of the tiny, cramped interview room. She sat as they rearranged themselves behind her, then pulled one of her daughters to her side. Shyly, the girl looked up at me.

"You have lovely children," I said.

The girl pressed her mother's arm and giggled. The other children smiled. They were astonishingly beautiful. The older girls were long-limbed, graceful, shy. They hung behind, stood by the door, crouched down to the younger children, whispered to them and made them laugh. The smaller children were bright, mischievous, affectionate. There were six children aged between three and fourteen, and the baby in Ayaan's arms.

Ayaan told me why she had left Somalia, stroking her baby's cheek, tucking the blanket around his face. I typed up everything she said. She was, she told me, from a minority, powerless clan. Most of my Somali clients were. In Somalia, minority clan members were regularly abused and persecuted by more powerful clans. The lowest clans were considered "untouchable," dirty and inhuman. This random, hateful classification by clan was one of the parts of the stories I heard that I found hardest to understand.

Ayaan's father had taken a job in security with the Government of the dictator Said Barre. A few years after the Government was overthrown in 1991, men loyal to the new leader, General Aidid, murdered Ayaan's father and brothers because of their connection to the old regime.

A few years later, Ayaan's husband, who was also from a minority clan, was shot and killed when he resisted demands for money by men from another, more powerful clan. Ayaan was pregnant with their second child, a girl, at the time. Her daughter, Lul, was two years old. She and her sister would never get to know their father.

Ayaan's children were quiet as she spoke. The baby was sleeping. One of the younger girls was leaning over Ayaan's shoulder, humming to him, smoothing his hair.

Ayaan, worried that the men who killed her husband would come after her, made her way to the Somali coast. Boats were taking people fleeing Somalia across the gulf to Yemen. Heavily pregnant, Ayaan boarded one of these boats with Lul. In Yemen, she followed others to a refugee camp. Her daughter Marian was born soon after, in a makeshift clinic in the camp. When Marian was six weeks old, Ayaan asked people in the town for work. She found a job as a housemaid and was allowed, with her two children, to sleep on the floor of the garage next door to the house she cleaned.

Soon, Ayaan told me, she met a man called Musab, a Somali refugee from another minority clan. They got married when Ayaan's daughter Marian was one year old. They lived in Yemen for seven years and had four children together. One, a son named Abdul, died from malaria when he was six weeks old.

Ayaan paused, and I stopped writing, then read what I had written. I had noted the death of Ayaan's son without even being aware it. My notes said: *Son, Abdul, died at six weeks. Malaria.* The 'A's in 'Malaria', I had filled with ballpoint ink when Ayaan had stopped talking and brought her waking baby to her breast. I hadn't registered her son's death. *Her son's death.* It was just one more tragedy to add to the list of tragedies in her life. Statistically, it was to be expected. Almost twenty percent of children in Somalia died before the age of five. The refugees I worked with who had several children had almost always lost at least one. I would ask, as a matter of course, *How many living children do you have? How many have died?* That at least one had died could reasonably be assumed.

Why would the pain Ayaan experienced upon losing her child be less because she had already lost so many others in her life? The idea was, of course, absurd. And yet, I had already seen, it permeated long-term staff's thinking, and now, I feared, mine. A refugee's loss is not the same as ours. This is why we don't have to feel so bad for them or worry about treating them with more compassion. *They're used to it.*

One morning, Ayaan told me, her husband Musab went to the market, and by dark still hadn't returned. Two days later, his body was found in a house; he'd been beaten and strangled with wire. Musab's brother told Ayaan that the men who had killed him were Somali, but from a majority clan. Musab had owed them money when he lived in Somalia, and when the men discovered him living in Yemen, they demanded he pay it back. Musab couldn't pay the money and kept asking for more time. When the men realized he would never be able to pay it, they beat and strangled him to death.

Ayaan told me her story quietly, her voice wistful, but resigned. Her father and brothers, and now both of her husbands, had been murdered. Her son had died when he was six weeks old.

Ayaan appeared to be around my age. As a single white woman in Africa, I took boda bodas to expat parties on Friday and Saturday evenings and spent Sundays at the pool. I drank Waragi, a local gin that came in sachets like fast-food ketchup. I went to bars and danced to Toto's "Africa" and Shakira's "Hips Don't Lie." If I wanted, I could leave Uganda when I wished, move on, find another post.

I didn't understand how Ayaan was even here, sitting before me. I didn't know how much horror, how much grief, one person could endure.

Ayaan's baby stirred in her arms, and two of her daughters fought to lift him up. The bigger girl succeeded and held him against her shoulder. The younger girl stroked his cheek, testing if he was really awake. He blinked, and she smiled at him, tickled his chin, rubbed her forehead against his.

After the murder of her second husband, Ayaan made her way to Uganda and stayed in a refugee camp. There, she met a refugee from Ethiopia, who helped her and was kind to her children. They fell in love, but other Somalis warned the man not to marry her. They told him that since Ethiopian troops were in Somalia to help overthrow the new Islamic rulers, Ethiopians were the enemies of Somalis. When they learned that Ayaan was pregnant with his baby, they issued death threats against him, and he fled. Ayaan never heard from him again. He was the third partner she had lost.

I looked at Ayaan's children. A boy with freckled milky brown skin rubbed the hem of his sister's skirt between his fingers and sucked on his thumb. I waved at him, and he pulled his hand from his mouth, waved back with a shy smile, then returned his thumb to his mouth. Ayaan gestured to him and said, "Somalis disowned me because of him – because I have an Ethiopian child." She lifted the boy onto her lap, and he pulled his thumb from his mouth again and smiled and kissed her cheek. Ayaan absently untangled his curls. She looked up suddenly, and said, her voice low, "I need to talk to you alone."

I nodded, and she spoke to the eldest girl, who ushered the others outside. The youngest went running, chasing each other, laughing; one girl catching another by her braids. Ayaan waited until they'd all dispersed into the yard. She leaned forward, looking at me intently, and said, "I have seven children to support."

I looked out to the children, the youngest still giggling, the older girls playing with the baby, tiptoeing his feet along the ground, pretending to make him walk.

"It is very hard," she told me. "None of my children are at school. They want to learn! The biggest girl worked for other Somalis before as a maid. Now no one wants her when they learn that she's my daughter."

Ayaan rearranged her headscarf and tucked stray strands of hair underneath. She sighed. "I have to feed my children."

I nodded, not understanding, biting on the lid of my pen. She stayed silent then looked to the window. "Abdullahi, the baby – "

She gazed at her hands, then into my eyes. "I don't know who his father is. I don't even know if he's Somali." She paused, then lowered her eyes again. "The only way we can survive is if I take money for sex."

I placed my pen on the table. I hadn't guessed, hadn't expected to learn this.

"You're working as a sex-worker?"

Ayaan nodded and looked away. "Abdullahi's father was one of my clients. I don't know which. Some are Somali men, some Ethiopians. If other Somali men learn what I'm doing, they will stone me to death."

I gazed at her. I knew that her fears were valid. Somali women I'd worked with had been ostracized and punished for much less. One woman I'd worked with had been completely isolated because she had fecal incontinence as the result of a fistula. The fistula was sustained during childbirth and was the result of the genital mutilation – the removal of the labia and clitoris, and sewing up of the vagina – she, like almost all other Somali women, had undergone as a girl.

"I can try to get you financial assistance," I told Ayaan, not knowing what else to say. "It's not much, but you should receive a small amount every month. I hope it's enough that you can stop doing this work."

I felt a wave of guilt, like nausea, when I thought about the tiny amount she would receive if she received anything at all. Though senior staff earned six-figure salaries, many acted as though they were doing refugees a favor by granting them assistance of $40 a month, like they should be *grateful* for receiving such a tiny fraction of what they received. I too felt good sometimes – generous, even – when I secured financial assistance for – *bestowed it upon* – a refugee.

Ayaan nodded, not meeting my gaze. "Thank you, my sister."

I continued, "But we also need to find you another country that will take you and your children in. You can't keep living like this. I will submit your case to the US, but that will take months. Maybe a year or more." I spoke quietly. "I hope the money will help until then."

Ayaan brought her hands to her face and said, shaking her head, "I wish I had some way to thank you."

"No," I said too loudly, then more quietly, "This is my job."

She looked to her lap, "But I feel bad that I cannot thank you for what you've done."

From outside, we heard Abdullahi suddenly begin to cry. Ayaan and I stood and looked out. The bigger girls, it appeared, were arguing over who should hold him, who could calm him down. Ayaan rapped the window and beckoned. Reluctantly, her eldest daughter left the other girls and came with Abdullahi to the outhouse. Ayaan took the baby and waved her daughter back out. She rocked him, and his breath became less frantic, quiet, his cries swallowed up in little gasps.

I said, "Your children are beautiful."

Ayaan leaned toward me and said, indignantly, "I was beautiful too when I was young!"

I pulled the lid from my pen with my teeth and asked, "Ayaan, how old are you?"

She responded, "Thirty-six."

"You're young now!"

She shook her head and sighed. "Now I am just living for these ones."

She gestured to the window then rubbed the baby's back, holding him to her chest.

I told her, "I'm thirty-one. Do you think that's old?"

Ayaan didn't answer but continued patting the baby, rocking slightly from side to side. She hummed into his hair, then asked, "Do you have a husband?"

I told her, "No."

She rubbed her chin on the baby's head then looked up. "I will pray for Allah to send you one."

I laughed, bemused that, after the grief she had sustained from the men in her life, she still felt that my life was lacking without a husband. She leaned forward, her expression grave. "This is the only way I can thank you for what you've done. Every day I will pray."

I tried to look serious, not wanting to offend her, and said, "Thank you."

Ayaan kissed her baby's head loudly, wetly, causing him to giggle, revealing two tiny teeth in the middle of his lower gum. She called her children back in, and they lined up to shake my hand. One of the girls had been redoing her sister's braids, and she twisted the braid in a knot and held it in place while she shook my hand. Ayaan held my arm and smiling conspiratorially, whispered, "My sister, I will pray for you."

I nodded, thanking her, not thinking that I might recall her words soon, and wonder, even if I was an atheist, if her prayers had been heard.

Prayer

By now, I had worked with refugees whose whole families had been killed in front of them, and young men who had been forced to rape their mothers in front of their fathers. I didn't know how any of them survived. I often thought of Martha and of other people I knew who had died by suicide. I thought of my own depression. I hadn't endured anything like Ayaan or many of the people I worked with had, but I still found it difficult, sometimes, to move forward. From the stories of the people I worked with, I tried, always, to piece together the puzzle of how to survive.

Religion, I knew, was part of it. A Ugandan doctor had asked me if I was religious, if I believed. I told him, no, I was an atheist. He looked at me with contempt. "Maybe if you had faith, you wouldn't be so depressed."

Outraged, I reported him to the head of the clinic, a British man, who agreed the Ugandan doctor had been out of line, and said he would speak to him, and tell him not to say things like this again. But I knew that what he said was true. I wasn't a believer. I would never be. But if I had the faith that many of my clients had, the conviction that everything was part of God's plan, I was certain I would feel more at peace.

Every refugee I had worked with was religious – Muslim, Adventist, Catholic, Pentecostal, or Born Again. They asked God to bless me and told me they'd pray for me. In Somali and Sudanese interviews, it was the only thing I understood: I would hear "Allah something Allah" and I would know they were saying, "May God grant you a long life." Biblical references permeated refugees' accounts of their flights: "I was attacked, left unconscious by the road, then a Good Samaritan rescued me." When I would explain that the decision about resettlement would be made by the resettlement country, refugees nodded and smiled as though I was naive. They would correct me: "It's in God's hands now."

***

Papy was a refugee from eastern Congo, sixteen years old and Catholic. When he was playing football one day, a neighbor called for him and his two brothers to come home. The boys reached the house and were told their parents had been shot dead. The neighbors brought them inside, where their parents' bodies were still slumped on chairs. Papy's father had worked in the gold mines in Ituri and was from the Lendu tribe. The neighbors told the children that their parents had been shot by militia from the rival Hema clan. The militia had asked the boys' father to hand over gold, and shot him when he couldn't. Two days later, Papy and his brothers buried their parents outside their house. A month after this, Papy's eldest brother ran off to the bush to fight the militia who had killed his parents. Papy never saw him again. Papy and his other brother began to fear for their lives, and they fled Congo for Uganda. In Uganda, Papy and his brother lived in a church, then in a refugee settlement. After a year, Papy's brother left the settlement to look for work in another town and never came back. Papy posted signs at refugee organizations and asked other refugees from Congo, but no one had seen him since. Papy left the settlement to sleep on the floors of other refugees' houses in Kampala and live off their leftover food.

I told Papy that we would argue his case to be accepted by another country. He told me what he really wanted was help with finding his brother. I said we could only put a sign at the NGO where we met refugees, but he'd already tried that. We agreed that he'd put a sign up one last time. There was no response.

Papy told me his story, and I took notes and told him I'd meet him again. When I'd written up the resettlement application, I brought it back so he could read it and check that everything was correct. I told him we would submit it and hope that he would be accepted in the next few months. Papy told me he belonged to a prayer group that met every week to pray. He said he would pray for me, and asked me to pray for him. I put the lid on my biro and folded my notes in two. I said, "I'm sorry, I don't believe."

Papy looked at me, his eyes wide, devastated. He said, "Please, will you pray for me."

I said, "I will do everything I can to help you, but... I'm not the right person to pray for you. I don't believe. It would be better to ask someone who does." I was trying to shift the blame onto God – *He won't answer the prayers of a phony, he won't listen to someone who doesn't believe, or who doesn't believe he is good.*

Papy pushed his thumbs through the holes in his sleeves, then looked up, still crestfallen. He asked, "Why won't you pray for me?"

I said, "I will... hope for you."

He stared at me, then lifted the battered blue folder with his documents and left the room.

The weekend after I met Papy, I went with my friend to a bar by Lake Victoria. I told him what Papy had asked me. My friend put his drink down and said, "He's just a kid. He's been through enough already. You should have said that of course, you would say a prayer. You made him even more distressed. Why couldn't you just say you would pray for him?"

I tried to light a cigarette, but the flame died in the wind. I knew he was right. Why had I refused? Was upholding my integrity, or whatever it was, more important than comforting a child who had gone through – was still going through – hell?

I put the cigarette down and looked away. I said, "It's too late."

Out of Sight

I kept a set of local, handmade furniture: a bamboo sofa and matching armchair, and a small, low bamboo table, on the terrace of my house. The cushions on the sofa were covered in a cream fabric that was patterned with faded red hearts. On the table were old papers – Guardian Weeklies and New York Review of Books – that had yellowed and wrinkled in the sun.

In the evenings, I lay on the sofa on the terrace, reading, smoking cheap cigarettes, and listening to the call to prayer.

On Saturday mornings, I tended to the garden, pruning plants in a sunhat and mud-stained cut-off shorts. I planted tomatoes, cilantro, beans, and tall red and yellow flowers, whose names I never found out. On weekend afternoons, I brought out coffee and listened to the World Service on a tiny, battery-operated radio, and looked out to Lake Victoria. In these moments in the terrace and garden, I felt, in spite of the work, the darkness, the stories, a sort of exuberance, bliss.

A new colleague had joined the office, a woman called Laura. She was a few years older than I, and Australian. She worked in a different department to me, but still, on occasion, interviewed refugees. She was tall, tanned, and irreverent. This was her first UN post. She was good at her job, and as shocked as I was by the corruption she saw.

When a house in my compound became free, Laura moved in. On weekend mornings, we began to share breakfast – Ugandan coffee and pastries on one or other of our terraces.

On a Friday evening in early 2007, Laura came to my house, carrying a bag of tiny local limes. She sat on the armchair on the terrace, and I pulled myself off the sofa where I'd been reading and went inside. I brought back a bottle of Ugandan gin, tonic water, two glasses, a cutting board, knife, and tray of ice. I sliced lime on the board across the bamboo table and poured the gin and tonic. I dropped the lime into the glasses, then poked ice out from the tray. We sipped the drinks and watched the city lights come on over the hills, and from the dark patches, tried to guess which neighborhoods had no power. Lake Victoria was a dark hollow, like a semi-circle of black card pasted over the lights. We drank the gin slowly, smashed ice, and poured more. Laura stirred her lime with the knife. She sat back and said, "I had a refugee client today who was so hot."

I curled my legs up under me on the sofa, feeling warm now from the gin, and lit a cigarette. Fruitbats were shrieking overhead, circling the porch and landing with a clatter on the tin roof. "Where was he from?"

"Eritrea," Laura replied. "His name was "Israel." She took a long drink from her gin then shook the ice in the bottom of the glass. I thought about the Eritrean clients that I had. I didn't know him. *Israel.*

"I had a couple once," I told her, "– an Ethiopian man and a Somali woman. Other Somalis taunted the woman, saying her husband, who was Christian, was a Jew because he was Amharic. They said she was an affront to Islam. The woman was terrified because the other Somalis were insisting her partner was Jewish and saying she should be stoned to death. Then the couple had a baby boy. But do you know what they called him?" I paused. "Israel! Would you call your baby 'Israel' if you were receiving death threats because you'd been accused of marrying a Jew?"

Laura leaned back, looking up to the porch ceiling, and laughed. "This Israel was totally flirting with me. I had to stop myself from flirting back. And he was only twenty-four."

I smiled and drew deeply on the cigarette. I knew if other colleagues heard us, they would be appalled. I was glad for Laura; thankful to have someone to be honest about work with, relieved. I didn't know if I could have continued in the job if she hadn't been there.

"I've had some hot clients," I told her. I mean, I've interviewed them."

Laura smirked. "Which nationality do you prefer?"

I told her that I didn't have a preferred nationality, but I'd asked Ali to give me all the human rights defenders, the high-profile and political cases, the ex-prisoners of conscience. I said, "He's happy to give me those cases – he thinks it's just my area of interest. But really, it's like I'm using him as a dating agency."

Laura coughed and spat her gin on the ground.

I said, "Yes, he's kind of my filter."

Laura laughed. "Maybe I should get him to assign me all the Ethiopians and Eritreans. They always have interesting backgrounds."

I nodded. "Some of them – do you remember the judge?"

Laura said, "You liked the judge? You're sick."

I told her, "I liked his story. What he did. He spoke out and risked his life – that's really sexy."

Laura grimaced. "But he was old!"

I said, "Still sexy. And that guy – the Rwandan, who was in the Presidential Guard, and no country would accept him? Extremely dodgy, but sexy."

Laura pulled the lime from her glass and sucked on it. "No, he *was* sexy. Those shifty eyes. Did you believe his story?"

I shrugged. "I don't know."

We poured more gin and tipped in the rest of the ice, which was almost liquid.

"Do you remember," Laura asked me, "the game we played at the office retreat?"

I nodded, smiling, and lit another cigarette. We had played a game at the recent retreat, to teach us about sexual harassment. The irony that the office had covered up the actual harassment that had already taken place didn't seem to bother any of the management who took part. The Human Resources team who had organized the game did not even seem to be aware of the harassment that had occurred.

In the game, we were told we should all stand in the middle of the room. When a statement was called out, those who agreed should stand against the left wall, those who disagreed, against the right. The game-leader, a junior HR officer, had read, "I can have sex with a refugee as long as it doesn't influence how I handle their case."

Most of the staff moved across to the right, but a few – all men – went to the left. The leader asked someone by the right wall why she thought that was wrong. She replied, "To protect our reputation?"

The leader thought for a moment then said, "Well, that too. But it's because they are our beneficiaries, and so the relationship can never be equal. It would be an abuse of power."

Some of the people by the left wall had looked at her with contempt. Throughout the game, Ali had appeared embarrassed, and waited until he could see which wall most people had moved to before following them.

I asked Laura if she could imagine Ali having an affair with a refugee. She snorted. "He doesn't even think they're human. Though he thinks the little kids are cute. But do you know he told our Ugandan colleague that her kids were nice, but to him, black kids all look the same?"

I winced, remembering him saying the same thing to me. I knew Ali would never find a refugee attractive, except in a purely physical way. And perhaps not even that. It just wouldn't be possible for him to think about them as full people. Had he always been like this? Or had years of this work and operating in this world – with this amount of power – done this to him?

Laura cut a fresh slice of lime. I felt drunk. The Ethiopian judge *was* attractive. It wasn't sleazy, I told myself, that I was attracted to him – I would never act on it. He was sexy. I was only being honest by admitting that. And if I fantasized about clients in this way, I reasoned further, didn't that mean that I, unlike Ali, at least saw refugees as human? Didn't that separate me more from him?

I wondered whether our refugee clients talked about us in the evenings as we did about them. Once, a Congolese woman had told me that I was "well known" in the Congolese community. "Everyone know who you are," she had said. "They say you are nice, and softer than the other officers. They want to get you." I wasn't sure if "softer" was even supposed to be a good thing.

I looked out to the city. It was a clear night. I tried to name, in my head, the neighborhoods that were in darkness. The areas where the refugees lived, the slums, were always dark: no one there had electricity. Where Laura and I lived, on top of the hill, there was almost always power. The American Ambassador lived close to us and shared our electricity line. We benefitted from the lengths taken to ensure his power supply never went out. There was no malaria where we lived either: it was too high for malarial mosquitos to survive. In the valleys, in the areas where refugees lived, malaria was still a risk. I sucked on my cigarette, breathed out deeply and shut my eyes. When I opened them, the dark patches were no longer there; the blurred edges of the lights from neighborhoods with power blotted them out. If I kept my eyes unfocused, poured more gin, they would remain like that: fuzzy, obscure, out of sight.

In Your Hands

Peter had fled Southern Sudan sometime during the second Sudanese civil war, which lasted from 1983 to 2005. The war had been characterized by human rights abuses and marginalization of the mainly Animist and Christian African south of the country by the predominantly Muslim Arab government in Khartoum, fighting over natural resources between the north and south of the country, and clan-based conflict in the south. Around two million people had died as a result of the conflict, and four million had been displaced.

Peter lived now in a refugee settlement in northern Uganda. He was referred to me on emergency medical grounds. Though I worked mainly with urban refugees, I was occasionally assigned clients who lived in settlements, when they needed to be relocated to another country, urgently. These were almost always medical cases: refugees who suffered from serious illnesses that could not be treated in Uganda, and whose lives were threatened in the absence of treatment. Our quota for emergency medical cases was small, and was used only for those in direst need.

Peter came to his interview wearing a British postman's uniform: a short-sleeved blue shirt with the Royal Mail insignia stitched on the pocket in yellow and red. I imagined a postman wearing this shirt to deliver mail to suburban British letterboxes, and the journey the shirt must have taken to make its way from this to a Ugandan refugee settlement. Did a retired postman donate the shirt to charity? A disgruntled postman who'd lost his job? Some Western charities sent donated clothes that couldn't be sold at home to Africa: the cheap, donated clothes flooded the market and put local tailors out of business. In Nkhata Bay, Malawi, I had seen an elderly woman in a T-shirt that proclaimed, in flashy, neon lettering, *Batman Returns!* while a young man in nearby Mzuzu wore a shirt that advertised, surreally, the defunct Irish supermarket, Quinnsworth. Did Peter know what Royal Mail was? It was likely that he couldn't read – many Southern Sudanese refugees could not – and the insignia probably meant nothing to him. I pictured him as the postman, paid by Royal Mail to deliver letters in a faraway African refugee settlement.

Peter's medical report said he had a tumor in his eye that was spreading to his brain. Based on his medical report, his need for resettlement was obvious and easy to argue: the potentially lifesaving treatment he needed was not available in Uganda. The grounds for his refugee status were less clear. Like other Southern Sudanese who had fled during the civil war in Sudan, Peter had been accepted as a *prima facie* refugee in Uganda: the precise reasons why he, as an individual, was a refugee had not been established. For resettlement purposes, however, it was not enough that he had fled war; I would have to establish that he was a refugee according to the UN definition – that he had fled Sudan because of a well-founded fear of persecution based on his nationality, religion, race, political opinion or social group. I had arranged to interview him with an interpreter in order to obtain information from him that would allow me to make this case.

"When did you flee Sudan?" I asked Peter.

"I don't know," he told me through the interpreter.

"Then how old were you at the time?"

He put his hand to his head. His left eye was hugely protruding. He shrugged.

I thought for a moment, then asked him to show me how big he was when he'd left. He brought his hand down to his shoulder.

"Ten years old?" I guessed.

He nodded.

"And why did you flee?"

"Because my house was attacked," he told me, "and my son was killed."

I looked at my notes, then the interpreter. He was ten years old when he fled, but he already had a son who'd been killed? "How old were you when your son was killed?" I asked.

He shook his head. "I don't know."

I said, "I can't argue your refugee claim unless I know when you fled and why."

The interpreter turned to Peter and explained, slowly, what I had said. Peter looked distressed and replied at length.

The interpreter told me, "He doesn't know numbers. He hasn't been to school and can't count. He doesn't know how to answer the questions you're asking him."

"I understand," I said, "But his case won't go anywhere unless I can give an idea of when and why he left."

The interpreter turned again to Peter, who looked distraught. He asked me if I couldn't make an estimate of the year he fled myself. I shook my head.

"How old was your son who was killed?" I asked him.

"I don't know."

"Was he a baby? Was he walking? Was he a small child?"

Peter held his hand low in the air.

"Can I say that he was three?"

Peter raised his hand in a gesture of *whatever you like.*

"But if you had a three-year-old son at the time," I said, exasperated, "you can't have been ten years old." I placed my hand at my shoulder to demonstrate the size he'd told me he was.

Peter shrugged. I stared at him. Many of the refugees I worked with had no numeracy skills and no real idea of their age. Women with young children estimated themselves to be sixty; others had sons and daughters born, they said, four months apart. We, and resettlement countries, imposed numbers on them, unfairly, demanding dates of birth and events, and new officers would reject their claims when the figures didn't add up. I knew this, but still, Peter had to be able to give a better estimate of his age than to suggest that his son was born when he, himself, was a young child. I turned again to his file, to the notes I'd made. "How long had you been married when your son was killed?"

Peter looked surprised. His voice, when he replied to the interpreter, expressed indignation.

"He wasn't married," the interpreter told me. "He was still only a boy."

I put my pen down. I told the interpreter, "Please, I need your help. Can't you see it doesn't make sense that he left because his son was killed, if he himself was only a child when he fled?"

The interpreter spoke quietly. "He is not being uncooperative. Numbers mean nothing to him – he can't count, he doesn't understand."

I replied, the edge in my voice uncontrolled. "But you don't need to understand numbers to know that you couldn't have been a small child if you already had a son of about three years old."

The interpreter shrugged and translated what I had said. Peter looked at him, confused. He didn't speak. I said, "Ask him what age he is now. And how long he's been in Uganda."

Peter said he didn't know but had been told he was born in 1990. I looked at the interpreter. "1990?" This would make him sixteen or seventeen.

He repeated the number to Peter then laughed. "No – 1980. He was told he was born in around 1980."

I wrote it down then spoke directly to Peter. "And how long have you been in Uganda?"

Peter spoke, shaking his head. "A long time."

"Did you get married in Sudan or Uganda?"

Peter laughed. "Uganda."

"Then who was the mother of your son who was killed in Sudan?"

He looked bewildered by my train of thought and said, "My brother's wife."

I stopped writing. He had had a child with his brother's wife when he was ten years old? I re-read all of my notes. Finally, I looked up, understanding. "Peter, was this your son, or your brother's son who was killed?"

Peter spoke matter-of-factly. "My brother's son. But my brother was killed before. The boy grew up with me and my mother."

I drew a line through the word "son."

"So," I said, "The boy who was killed – it was your nephew."

The interpreter answered without consulting Peter, "But you know, in our culture it is the same. We call our brothers' children *our* children."

I looked back at the numbers, then addressed the interpreter. "Peter thinks he was born in 1980. He fled Sudan when he was around ten years old after his young nephew was killed in an attack on the family's house. Please ask him if I can write that he fled Sudan in around 1990."

The interpreter put the question to Peter, and he nodded noncommittally.

"Who attacked your house?" I asked. "How was your nephew killed?"

Peter shrugged again. "I don't know. I was too young."

This wouldn't help his case. I sighed. "What do you think would happen if you returned to Sudan now?"

"I won't be able to get medical treatment," he said, looking confused.

"But those aren't legal grounds for refugee status," I told him, my voice rising again. "You know I need to be able to argue that you fear persecution in Sudan, so the resettlement country will accept you as a refugee."

I looked at Peter, thinking, *Please understand what I'm saying. Just tell me what I – what they – need to hear. Please make something up, and I'll write it down. I will take you at your word.*

Peter pressed his hands to his forehead, then looked up. He spoke as though exhausted. "I fear this pain. There is no medical help for me in Sudan."

I stared at him. His eyeball looked like it was being propelled out with the force of a pinball spring. I closed my eyes. I thought, *Please no, I want to hit this man.*

I sat back and inhaled deeply. I could not contain my frustration, even if I knew it was not Peter that I was truly frustrated with, but myself, my role, this organization, this system. Resettlement was all we had to offer Peter; it was the only way I could help any of my clients. I was not convinced that resettlement was the solution, but we provided no alternative for those with life-threatening medical problems – no medical evacuation, where Peter could be flown abroad for treatment, and then return. Permanent overseas relocation was all we could offer him, and how could he afford, if he wished, to come back? I knew how difficult it would be for Peter would to cope in a Western country with no literacy or numeracy skills, no background in anything but subsistence farming. I hated the fact that I could book a plane ticket and receive medical treatment within days but Peter would wait months or longer, would perhaps never be resettled, or would be offered resettlement too late. A previous medical client, a young girl, had died before her case was processed. Another refugee was rejected for resettlement on medical grounds, and died in Uganda. From Peter's medical report, it was clear that he needed to receive treatment urgently. It was possible that he wouldn't be resettled in time. It was easy – *a relief* – to project my anger onto him, the victim of what I was actually angry about. I had done it with other refugees, I knew, already, many times. Anger – *you are the one who's in the wrong, not I, not we* – helped unburden me, and the other staff I heard expressing annoyance at refugees, of guilt. It was a relief too to question the worth of resettlement: then if my work was not good enough, if a client was not accepted for resettlement as a result, I could reassure myself by thinking, *who knows if it would have even helped?*

I leaned forward. "Peter, I need you to tell me the problems you had in Sudan, and the problems you would have if you returned."

He still looked uncomprehending. I shifted in my chair. I said to him slowly, deliberately, "Tell me about the attack on your family's home, how it would appear that your whole family was targeted, though they only managed to kill your nephew. Then tell me about how you would be at risk again if you returned. You will only be accepted if I can argue convincingly that you have reason to fear persecution if you were returned to Sudan. I need to argue that your fear is justified and real."

Peter stayed silent then nodded slowly, a look of first realization, then willingness to conspire, passing over his face. He concentrated for a few moments and I made as though I was re-reading my notes. He spoke to the interpreter, pausing now and then in thought.

"His nephew was killed," the interpreter began, "When a bomb was thrown at the house. The bomb was meant to kill the whole family. He heard through other refugees that the people who had tried to kill the family took over their land when they fled. If Peter returned to Sudan, he would be killed by the same people, who would fear that he had come back for revenge."

I nodded quickly and wrote this down. "Who were the people who killed your nephew?"

Peter reflected for a moment. "They could have been the Sudanese People's Liberation Army – the SPLA."

"Do you have particular reason to fear persecution at the hands of the SPLA?"

Peter nodded in understanding of what I was asking of him.

"When I was young, before I left Sudan, the SPLA tried to recruit me as a child soldier, but my mother refused to let me go. If I return to Sudan, I will be known to the SPLA and hated by them, as someone who refused to join their ranks. They will persecute me if I return." He smiled thinly, knowing that this was what I'd been looking for. I looked to the interpreter, but couldn't read his expression.

When I'd finished writing, I told the interpreter that Peter could go. The interpreter listened intently as Peter replied, then said, "He thanks you for your patience. He says his future is in your hands."

"No, it's not," I said quickly, "It's in the hands of the government of the resettlement country. You know I will argue your case, but I don't make the final decision."

The power I had over Peter's life and that of other refugees I worked with – the power to decide whether to submit a person for resettlement; the outcome, a new life on the other side of the world, relying on the effort I put into their case – had become too much to bear. If I was sick for a day and didn't work, a whole family might not be resettled. A person whose prospects might have been transformed, whose life might have been saved by resettlement, would have a different fate. If I took too long to submit a medical case, a person could die. Unable to bear the responsibility, I tried to convince myself that it lay elsewhere: with resettlement countries, or other staff, or even the refugees themselves.

The interpreter translated what I'd said, but Peter was impassive. I waited.

I told him, "I'm sorry about earlier. It's just – I want to help you, but the resettlement governments are very strict. I want them to accept you, but they won't if I can't present the kind of argument they understand."

Peter had one hand over his protruding eye, his fingers pressing his forehead hard as if trying to will away the pain. He looked tired, resigned, in pain.

I waited, wanting him to respond, to say it was fine, to absolve me of my role in all of this. He stood up, smoothed out the Royal Mail shirt, and left, not saying anything, his head still in his hands.

The Maid Will Do It Tomorrow

The first time I had seen how expats in Africa lived, I was staying with a friend in Mozambique. I was shocked when, after a dinner party at my friend's house, I was stopped from washing up: *The maid will do it tomorrow.* Laundry was taken from the bedroom – from the floor, if that's where it had been left – and returned, ironed, to hangers in the closet. Trash cans were emptied. Floors were mopped every day. We glided through the house, eating meals that were cooked for us, standing up at the end, leaving dishes on the table, knowing everything would be taken care of. There was nothing we needed to do. I felt uncomfortable at the outset. How could I just leave the dishes overnight for the maid to greet in the morning, knowing I'd enjoyed a dinner party and then left them for her? What would I do in my friend's situation, I wondered? Not employ anyone, and clean up my own mess? My friend laughed when I told her that. "That *isn't* helpful. Women regularly show up on my doorstep, pleading with me to employ them. People need work. Pay people a decent wage, treat them fairly. Don't deny them a job because of your own hang-ups."

***

In the house that I moved to after the Indians' house, I had my own housekeeper, Dorothy.

Dorothy was referred to me by my Rwandan neighbor, Raymond, who worked for UNDP. "She's not the best," he told me one evening in his house over gin. "Sometimes I'll leave a cup on a side table, and I'll come home to find it still there."

I squirmed and blotted a drop of condensation on my gin glass with my finger. Raymond described leaving the cup on a table as though it were a test. Dorothy had failed. I knew that Dorothy's employers could treat her as they wished: without dignity, without respect. They could test her, chastise her, or fire her if she failed. She had no choice but to accept it. Where would she turn?

I thought I could live with an occasional cup being left on a side table, but asked, "Is she trustworthy? You don't think she'd ever steal?"

Raymond shook his head with certainty. "I visited her home before I hired her. I wanted her to know that if she ever did anything, I knew where she lived. Then I took a photograph of her: she knows I can bring that to the police."

I looked away. I knew that Dorothy would be used to this attitude: she was powerless. There were few employment opportunities in Uganda. I had seen before how meekly housekeepers acted in front of their current and prospective employers.

"What," I asked Raymond, "is her house like?" He shrugged, as though it wasn't relevant. "Not good. You know. Very poor."

I hired Dorothy to clean my house three mornings a week. On those afternoons, she worked at Raymond's house, and on the other two days, somewhere else. She showed up each day early and impeccably dressed. She wore blouses and skirts that were ironed to perfection, and high-heeled shoes. She brought a plastic bag with cleaning clothes that she changed into after I left, and out of again after finishing cleaning the house. I wore flip-flops and strappy tops made from African fabric to work. Since I rode on the back of boda bodas to get to the office, I also often wore jeans. Dorothy would look me over each morning with scarcely hidden disdain.

Over time, I noticed when I came home after Dorothy had cleaned, that my house would smell of my perfume. I didn't wear perfume to work, so I knew it wasn't left over from the morning, and the scent was strong enough to suggest it had been freshly sprayed. *Was Dorothy spraying herself with my perfume before she left the house?* There was no other explanation. I began to notice other things: clothes that went missing, then, mysteriously, showed up again. One day as Dorothy washed my breakfast dishes before I left the house, I noticed she was wearing a bracelet that looked curiously like my own. "Dorothy," I asked her, "Is that bracelet *mine?*"

She looked to her wrist as though she hadn't been aware she was wearing a bracelet, then as if surprised, nodded. "Yes, yes, it is!" She slipped it off casually, passed it to me, and resumed her work. Another day, she showed up at my house wearing a tank top exactly like one that I'd been missing for weeks. I stared at her in disbelief. *Could that really be my top?* If she was borrowing my clothes, how could she show up wearing them *in front of me?*

I was too confused and embarrassed to say anything: the subject now felt too delicate to bring up.

I knew what Dorothy was being paid. She couldn't possibly have enough money to buy nice perfume, clothes or jewelry of her own. I could afford it. And with the clothes at least, she was returning them, clean and ironed. It was impossible to tell they had even been worn. I thought of the other expats I knew – European and African – and how some treated their housekeepers. I thought of Raymond, taking Dorothy's photo so she'd be too scared to ever steal from him. I thought of my last housekeeper, and my failure to tip him.

I didn't want to be like that.

I told Laura about the reappearing clothes and the perfume. Laura's own housekeeper, Joyce, was legendary amongst housekeepers. She commanded such a high fee that she employed a housekeeper herself – someone to clean her house while she was off cleaning expats' homes. She didn't suffer fools gladly. She reported on other housekeepers in the compound to their employers when she saw them slacking off. She regularly shouted at the guards – and reported on them too – if they weren't taking their role seriously enough. They were scared enough of her to pull themselves up from the shade of the avocado trees, where they normally lay, and stand, glaring resentfully, by the gate.

When I told Laura about Dorothy's actions, she laughed, and shook her head. "You're too soft. She's using your stuff and you're letting her get away with it? I would have fired her long ago."

"But what's the harm?" I asked. "She gives the clothes back eventually, and I won't miss some perfume."

Laura shrugged. "That's how it starts. You haven't set any boundaries – you don't know what she'll move on to next."

Though I was uncomfortable with Laura's insinuation, I decided, finally, to talk to Dorothy. I was still too embarrassed to confront her outright, so I settled instead on sending her a brief and ridiculous passive-aggressive text. *Dorothy,* I wrote, *it would be great if you didn't use my perfume, jewelry or clothes. Thanks and see you on Tuesday!*

Minutes after I sent the text, Dorothy rang. I didn't pick up. Ten minutes later, she rang again, then half an hour after that, then late, when I was already in bed. I didn't answer. I didn't know what to say to her, or how to say it. I wanted her to know that I knew, but I didn't want – was too cowardly – to talk about it with her.

When I next saw Dorothy, she didn't mention the text message. My clothes stopped going missing, and I never smelled the perfume again.

***

In March of my second year in Uganda, my mother came to visit. She stayed in my house. She made fun of me for how spoiled I'd become, lifting my legs up while sipping coffee on the sofa, so Dorothy could sweep under my feet. I had asked her to bring Dorothy a present – a shirt, something decorative and glitzy, I thought, something brighter than her normal clothes, which were, I supposed, all she could afford. She brought a lime green T-shirt emblazoned with an image of a tropical beach, and the word *Vegas* inscribed unexpectedly above it in glittery font. Dorothy opened it, nodded and thanked both of us, and folded it into her handbag. Weeks later, returning home because I'd forgotten something, I found her wearing it to clean the house.

My mother asked Dorothy questions about her daughter, and she answered politely, in as few words as possible. Dorothy's daughter lived with her and Dorothy's mother, but her father, we gathered, wasn't on the scene. In her phone calls home, my mother told my youngest brother about Dorothy and her daughter, and about how little she imagined her daughter had. My brother's seventeenth birthday was coming up. After one of these calls, he sent a text message to my mother: *I don't really need anything for my birthday this year. You can use the money you would have spent on me to buy a present for the cleaner's daughter instead.*

On our next trip to the Indian-owned mall where expats and a few rich locals shopped, we went to the toy store with fifty dollars to spend on my brother's behalf. We bought sketch pads with shimmery pink covers, glitter markers, a white plastic doll like a Barbie (the store only sold white dolls), a bead set for making jewelry, a packet of modeling clay, and a purple and red plastic wallet. My mother put 10,000 shillings – three dollars – in the wallet, explaining that it was bad luck to give a purse with no money. I peeled off the price tags and wrapped the gifts in shiny gold paper, with a gaudy pink stick-on bow.

I gave the package to Dorothy, and explained that it was a gift from my brother to her daughter. She accepted it, looking confused. When she next came to my house, my mother had already left. She brought a card in a sealed envelope. The card bore an image of a fluffy yellow chick and the inscription "Easter Greetings." Inside, in large, studied cursive, was written,

To my auntie and her mama.

Thank you very much for the present. May God bless you this Easter and keep you safe.

From Angeline.

When I'd read it, Dorothy told me, "She enjoyed so much. Thank you and please send your thanks to your mother."

For a moment I thought she was going to cry. I regretted not buying Angeline more: I knew that she probably had few other toys. And what was another fifty dollars? One or two sushi meals at the Japanese restaurant? A night of drinks and taxis at the Irish bar?

On Hold

The waiting area at the NGO where we conducted interviews was the yard in front of the building. There were rows of wooden benches under the shade of a tin roof, but they didn't hold everyone who came. Those who arrived too late for a seat gathered in the shade of a mango tree, and when there was no shade left, on the ground in the sun.

A plastic box held donated toys for the children to play with while they waited. There were eyeless dolls, a blackboard with no chalk, and teddy bears with stuffing poking out of their torn seams. Younger children played quietly with these, while babies slept on their mothers' backs. In mango season, older children would search for long sticks with which to nudge the branches and knock the plump fruit down.

No matter the time of the scheduled interview, everyone showed up first thing in the morning. In part this was because few people had a watch or phone with which to tell the time, and they feared missing an interview that might lead to resettlement; in part it was because there was nothing else to do. Eventually, staff stopped allocating interview times at all, and simply assigned a day. Those whose interviews took place in the evening would spend up to eight hours sitting outside, waiting in the sun.

In May 2007, I was assigned to interview Samuel and his family, who had fled from the eastern Democratic Republic of Congo. They had been in Uganda for two years by then, and already been interviewed by my colleagues three times.

The Democratic Republic of Congo had endured years of human rights abuses and conflict under the crazed and brutal colonial ruler, King Leopold II of Belgium, and megalomaniac post-independence leaders including the infamous, leopard-skin-hat-wearing Mobutu. In neighboring Rwanda, the mainly-Hutu Interahamwe forces had slaughtered close to a million Tutsis in the genocide of 1994. When a new Tutsi regime was installed in Rwanda following the genocide, ex-Interahamwe Hutus, fearing reprisal, fled across the border to eastern Congo (then Zaire), fueling war there. Battle for resources in the region, including coltan – used in cell phones and other electronic devices – compounded the conflict. Though they didn't receive much international coverage, over five million people had died as a result of the wars in eastern Congo. Many of the worst stories I had heard – of torture, sexual violence, and even cannibalism – were from Congolese refugees.

On the morning of his family's scheduled interview, I called Samuel's name out into the NGO's yard. From the file, I understood that the family was French-speaking, and so I wouldn't need an interpreter.

Samuel stood and gestured to the rest of his family – his wife, his teenage daughter and two teenage sons – who were huddled in a small spot in the shade. He ushered them ahead of him and towards the building.

I stepped forward and stopped him. "I need to speak to you alone."

Samuel looked from me to his wife, then back. "Can my wife stay?"

I shook my head.

He looked hesitant, confused. I smiled apologetically, and waited for his family to return to their spot under the mango tree. I needed to speak to them individually, to check that their stories matched up.

The interview room was hot and stuffy. If I opened the window, the rows of people waiting outside would be able to hear us, so I kept it shut. Samuel looked uneasy. He kept casting around as if looking for his family, then finally sat down. He was wearing a shirt and pants in matching fabric. The shirt was button-up but collarless. The fabric was a thin grey cotton that had become shiny with wear.

I placed his file on the desk. It unsettled dust, which caused me to sneeze. Samuel said "Salut!" – *bless you!* – under his breath and I smiled. I read through the file, then pulled the laptop from my bag, opened a new document, and prepared to type.

"Why did you flee from eastern Congo?" I asked. The story was in his file, but I needed him to tell it to me again, to check that he was consistent.

Samuel nodded and inhaled deeply as though about to recite a rehearsed speech. "We were living in Goma, North Kivu. I'm a tailor. I taught tailoring to young boys – adolescents – at a school there. Laurent Nkunda's rebels were recruiting young male Tutsis in the area at the time. They told them that they would be paid well for joining, and threatened and punished them if they refused. Many of my students were forced to join."

I was familiar with Laurent Nkunda, a Tutsi rebel leader in eastern Congo. He claimed to be acting on behalf of the Tutsis who were under attack by ex-Interahamwe Hutus, while he and his troops were themselves alleged to have committed child abduction, pillaging of villages, murder, and rape.

Samuel looked to the window. There were children playing a game of chase just outside, but his family was out of view. "One of my students," – he followed a line scraped on the desk with his fingernail – "he refused to join. He was only twelve. Two days after he refused, Nkunda's soldiers came to his house, and raped his fifteen-year-old sister as punishment." He paused, staring at the line on the desk. "They did it in front of him." He exhaled loudly then tugged at the top of his shirt, as though it was constricting his breath. "Soon after, the boy disappeared. Nkunda's men must have taken him."

I returned to his notes. The story so far corresponded with what he had told my colleagues.

"After this happened, I went to the office of a local human rights organization. I spoke to the director and told him about the boys in my school, the forced recruitments into Nkunda's army, and the punishments of those who'd refused to join. Then I told them about the boy who had disappeared, presumably abducted. The organization asked me to speak on the radio about this, as a warning to other families to protect their young sons. I agreed that I would speak, if I could avoid using my name or saying where I worked. The next day, I recorded a statement about boys being threatened, punished, and abducted, after refusing to work for Nkunda."

Samuel looked down to his lap. He rubbed at a stain on the knee of his trousers, though it looked like it had long dried in. "My statement was played on a news feature about Nkunda the next day on Radio Goma." He licked the tip of his finger absently and rubbed again at the stain. "The rest of the week I worked. On the Saturday –" he stopped rubbing and looked up. He turned and gazed out the window. "I've already told your office what happened next."

I nodded. "I know. I'm sorry, but I need you to tell me again."

He picked up a Bic pen that was lying on the desk, tapped it against his cheek, then let his hands drop. "On the Saturday evening, I was at home with my family when there was a knock at the door. My wife opened it. She thought it was her sister, who had said she might visit with her children. There was a scream. I ran to see what had happened. At the door were four men, all armed with rifles." Samuel shook his head. "Two of the men ran in and grabbed me. My wife was still screaming, and one of the men hit her on the head with his rifle, to get her to stop. Then they marched me to a pick-up truck, blindfolded me, tied my arms and legs, pushed me onto the back, and threw a plastic sheet over me. One of the men sat on the back of the truck to guard me, and we left."

"Where did they bring you?" I asked.

Samuel shrugged. "We drove for about an hour. When we arrived, we were at a deserted building, with armed guards outside. They threw me into a room, where there was already another man. He was lying in the corner. Before they left, the men beat me with their rifles and said they would teach me not to speak out again." He paused, looking around. "I still don't know how they knew it was me on the radio. I just made the recording at the human rights office, and they dropped the tape off at the station. No one at the radio station even knew it was I. But," he added, quietly, "I learned later that someone from the human rights office had been kidnapped and punished too."

"How were you punished?" I asked him, checking against his notes.

He sighed. "The next morning they returned and beat me again with their guns. They kept pushing their guns to my head and telling me my time was up. They kicked me over and over, and slammed my head against the concrete floor. They told me that they were going to kick me to death and throw my body outside, to be eaten by the flies. They brought me outside twice a day to relieve myself, and otherwise I was left in that room."

"And the man who was being held with you?"

"He was also beaten. He was there because he'd stopped his son from working for Nkunda, and told his neighbors not to let their sons go."

"And how did you escape?"

His eyes were focused somewhere else as he spoke, in the distance, beyond the window, outside. "The other man had already been there for a week. He knew all the guards' habits. He told me that the night guard usually fell asleep for a while in the middle of the night – he could hear him snore. The lock was flimsy and by pushing hard once, we could break it. Then we needed to creep out around the guard, to the back of the building, and flee into the bush. That night, we did it. The guard didn't even stir."

"And how," I asked him though the answer was in his file, "did you get back home?"

"We spent the night walking through the bush. By the morning we'd reached a road, and we walked until a bus came that could take us to Goma."

"And when you reached your home?"

"That was it. I had to take my family and leave. Nkunda's men would have killed us all. We threw everything we could into some bags, and left on foot. We crossed the border at Bunagana and made our way here."

"And now?" I asked, "Where are you living? How are you supporting yourself?"

He shrugged. "I found a job – as a waiter. I work for an Indian man, in his café. It's not enough money to send my kids to school, but it's more than most refugees have. Still," he added after a moment, "I'm afraid, because I know there are supporters of Nkunda in Uganda. I saw one of his top men here just last week. When they're being pursued by Congolese soldiers, sometimes they flee across the border, stay in Uganda for a while, then go back. I'm afraid of one of them attacking me here, or kidnapping me and bringing me back to Congo." He paused, then added quietly, "Nkunda would reward them well."

I read back over my notes. Everything was consistent with what Samuel had told us before. I closed his file, satisfied, and walked outside with him to where rows of people were still awaiting interview. The shade had shifted, and Samuel's family were now sitting, squinting, in the sun. I asked his wife, Francine, to follow me inside.

Francine spoke quietly, hesitantly, looking around after every few words, as though to check someone else hadn't slid, unbeknownst to us, into the room. Her headdress, blouse and skirt were cut from the same fabric. It was orange with white splashes, thin black zigzags, and large deep blue and yellow swirls. The top was grandly conceived, with wavy blue brocade edging the neck and hem. The sleeves were long and cornet-shaped, draping low at the ends. The skirt fell in heavy folds from tucks pinched evenly about the waist. The outfit belied Francine's timidity, her anxious voice.

I asked her to tell me why she had fled from Congo, and she nodded and smoothed out the folds of the skirt. She told me the story of her husband's abduction, speaking quickly, deliberately, as though she'd practiced saying it many times. After describing his return from captivity, she looked around, then down to her lap. "There is something I haven't told you before. Something my husband doesn't know."

She worried a piece of brocade that had come undone from her blouse then looked around again. "The day after they took my husband, two of Nkunda's men, armed with rifles, came again to the home. First, I was confused, and thought they'd also come to take him. I told them, 'They've already taken him, he's gone, look, you can search the house.'" She sighed. "They laughed in my face. They said, 'It's not your husband we've come for,' and I thought – I thought my worst nightmare was going to come true: they were going to take my boys. But," she looked away, her face contorted, "it turned out that wasn't it, and there were nightmares that were maybe even worse." She stared down at her lap, and traced one of the spirals in the fabric with her finger. "They pulled Flora, my girl, from the other room and then pulled the boys in too." She shook her head. "I tried to stop them, but they had guns. One of the men pointed his rifle at me and the boys if we tried to move or look away. She pressed her hands to her eyes, "They took it in turns to defile my daughter."

I stared at her. "They raped her?"

She nodded, then added quietly, "They made me and my sons watch."

I looked through my notes. Flora was only fifteen. I asked, "Why didn't you tell us this before?"

Francine nodded as though expecting the question. "My husband isn't aware. I don't want him to know this happened."

"But my colleague spoke to you alone before, and you said nothing to her."

Francine looked to the window. "I didn't want to talk about it then."

I was unconvinced. Most of my clients emphasized the worst that had happened to them, in the belief, usually correct, that this would increase their chances of resettlement. Leaving the worst out – this never happened. It was more likely, I suspected, that another refugee had told Francine that *she* had been accepted for resettlement after telling us how her daughter had been raped, and Francine thought a similar story might work for her.

"And why do you want to tell us this now?" I asked.

She looked down. "I want you to know everything that happened."

I sat back, turning the pages in her file. When she had been asked in a previous interview whether anything had happened while her husband was gone, she had answered, "No."

"Could I speak with your daughter?" I said finally.

Francine shrugged. *Ça va.* "It's OK."

We left to fetch her daughter Flora, still sitting outside on the ground with her brothers. She shook her dress out as she stood up. It was handmade too, a sundress that came just below her knees. The fabric was brown, and patterned with a yellow radio motif. Between the radios were black music notes, jaunty quavers and swirly treble clefs.

Flora sat next to her mother. I said, "I'm sorry to have to ask you about this."

She looked down to her hands, folded on her lap.

"I just need to know everything that's happened, to help your family's case."

She stayed silent, not looking up.

"I have to ask you a few questions, which will be difficult. I'm not a counselor, but there is a counselor here, and if you want, I can bring you to meet her when we're done. You can make an appointment to talk to her, and she will try to help you."

Flora didn't move, didn't nod.

"Can you tell me what happened after your father was taken from your home in Congo?"

She answered after a moment, without looking up. "I was raped. Two men came. They both raped me. My mother and brothers had to watch."

Her voice was detached, as though she was reading from text in a language she didn't understand.

I asked her if she wanted to see the counselor. She looked to her mother then shook her head. I wrote the counselor's name on a sheet of paper, tore it off and passed it to her. "If you want to see her, you just need to make an appointment at the reception. You can do it any time. Please think about it." I hesitated. "Don't be worried or embarrassed. She deals with cases of sexual violence all the time."

I fumbled, hearing my words, hearing them sound more belittling than reassuring. Flora's expression didn't change. She folded the paper in two, and kept it clasped tight in her fist as she left the room.

I left the interview room after her, locked it, and walked to the back of the building. Bricks littered the ground: debris from renovations a few years before. A wooden box, painted UN blue and labeled "Suggestions," lay abandoned by the drain. I sat on a block of concrete against the wall and lit a cigarette. I thought of Francine and of her daughter in her music-notes dress. Why had they not told us before that she'd been raped? Why had his wife previously said "no," when we asked if anything had happened while her husband had been gone? Were they too traumatized, ashamed? I thought back to other clients I'd had. No one had held back information about being raped. It was so widespread; when a woman from eastern Congo *hadn't* been raped, I was almost surprised. It was, horribly, too common to be in any way taboo. Yet Flora and her mother had been interviewed four times and never mentioned it. I thought of Flora's silence, the lack of emotion. Wouldn't she be more distressed?

I returned to the interview room and opened the file once again. Other than the rape, everything in the story matched up with what the family had told us before. Now they had been living in Uganda, in poverty and unable to pay for the children to attend school, for two years.

From the window, I could see the rows of people still waiting to be seen. A woman seated on the front bench had laid her baby to sleep at her feet. The family beside her had been there since early morning, before the office had even opened, and the man held his head in his hands, his elbows propped on his knees. His daughters sat on the ground, the older one braiding and re-braiding the younger's hair. Behind them, a boy had pulled an armless doll from the box, and was walking it along the ground. A mother breastfed her baby, her eyes closed, humming.

I looked at the file. Four interviews, not mentioning a rape? It didn't make sense.

I thought back to a family we'd had once, a Somali family, who'd been refugees in Uganda for five years. They came for interview over and over, but were never found to qualify for resettlement. Finally, one day they came with their three-year-old daughter and told us she had been raped in the camp by a refugee from a rival clan. It was evidence, they said, that they weren't safe and needed to be resettled. It was clear too, they argued, that their daughter's trauma warranted a fresh start in a new place. The doctor's examination confirmed that the child had been raped, but something wasn't right. The doctor spoke to the child, then interrogated the family. The child hadn't been raped by another refugee in the camp, it emerged finally. She had been penetrated, using an object, by her parents, who wanted us to think she'd been raped, so we'd give them a chance at a new life in the West.

Samuel had told us the story about being kidnapped four times and his family was still here, with no future. He couldn't safely return to Congo, and Uganda could not provide the services or environment he needed to recover from his trauma. Even without his daughter's rape, he was eligible for resettlement. But if I submitted his case now, I wondered, would it inspire others to lie – to exaggerate their story for a better chance of resettlement? Would it penalize those who *didn't* lie? Would it encourage more families – like the couple who had *penetrated their daughter with an object* – to actually make their lives worse in order to be resettled?

I pushed open the laptop and stared at the blank screen. What would I do if I were in Samuel's family's situation – living in poverty in Uganda, not able to become a citizen there, not able to send my kids to school? What would I do if I saw hundreds of other families leave for a potentially better future – some of them after exaggerating what had happened to them, or making it up? Would I lie?

Samuel's file was already more than an inch thick. I could type up my notes from the interview and add to it, explaining why I wasn't sure I believed Francine's story. I would then put the case on hold. Samuel or his wife would likely approach us again in the future, try to argue their case, try even to *make their lives worse* in order to become stronger candidates for resettlement. Or I could submit them now.

Perhaps Francine and Flora were even telling the truth: I had no way to know for sure. Did it matter what I believed? Couldn't I give them, as was our policy in the absence of good reason not to, the benefit of the doubt?

I turned back the file's blue cover. Immediately inside was a page with the family's biographical information, with passport-sized photos of each person stapled to the top. I scanned it. Under Samuel's occupation, it stated "tailor." I thought back to his wife and daughter's elaborate outfits, and realized suddenly: *he must have made them*. I pictured him stitching them carefully, with a fabric and style of their choosing. I imagined him in his old life, teaching tailoring to whole classes of boys, and now, waiting tables in an Indian man's café. Would that be it?

I opened the file, tapped the laptop mouse, and brought the screen to life.

I typed up the family's story. I wrote that Flora, as a survivor of violence and severe trauma, required specialist psychological services not available in Uganda. She and her family's chances of recovery would be best, I argued, if they could be resettled to a country where such care was available, and where they could start a new life. When I'd finished, I read what I'd written, staring at it the words until they blurred into one another on the harsh, bright screen. I attached the document to an email recommending resettlement, and then pressed *send.*

Tell Me Why You Fled

Bereket arrived two hours early for his interview at the local NGO. He sat on a bench in the waiting area outside, looking around, his foot tapping the ground nervously. When I had finished my other interviews, which had gone over time, I called to him. He had been waiting now for almost three hours. He stood up quickly and followed me to the interview room. He shook my hand hard and thanked me. He was clutching a plastic folder with his documents. We sat down. I opened his file and checked that we had all of his biodata. I began, as I always began the main part of the interview, "Tell me why you fled."

Bereket told me that he belonged to the Oromo clan, a clan that had, for more than a hundred years, endured discrimination and persecution in Ethiopia. Like many Oromo men, he had been accused by the Ethiopian Government of supporting the Oromo Liberation Front, a group that promoted and fought for Oromo rights. As a result, he had been arrested and tortured three times in the twelve years before he fled. In captivity, he had been forced to spend days jumping in a squatting position up a slope. At other times, he was made to roll naked in sharp stones until he bled. To keep him afraid, he was forced to look at the corpses of those who had been killed before him. His captors raped his wife, and she contracted HIV, which she later passed to him. His wife had died two years before he fled to Uganda, and he was ill now, and alone.

The imagination of torturers was the element of refugees' stories that always disturbed and bewildered me most. I thought of them trying to come up with the most awful, painful, degrading forms of torture they could, and the idea that they went to such lengths – searched their imaginations for the ways they could hurt a person most – was sometimes more upsetting to me than even the many killings and rapes I heard about every day. The torture wasn't always, or even usually, to obtain information. Mostly it was a sadistic punishment: for being of the wrong political opinion or clan. Another Oromo man I worked with was made to lie on the ground with his eyes kept forcibly open for hours at a time, staring at the sun, unable to blink. Who had thought of that? What other potential means of torture had they rejected – *that one won't cause quite enough distress* – until settling upon this? Yet another had been forced, during months of captivity, to do work that was deliberately pointless, like digging deep holes just to fill them in again. The more pointless the labor, the greater he would be frustrated and humiliated by it.

The worst story I had heard was of a woman who had been held hostage by a cannibal sect in eastern Congo. As punishment for her husband belonging to a rival militia, her baby was killed in front of her. She was forced to cook, and eat, his remains. How did the captors feel when they came up with that? How did they feel when they carried it out, when they made this woman watch her own baby be killed, then, with a machete to her head, watched her cook and eat him? Did they observe this with satisfaction? With glee? At what point in their lives had they stopped being human if this, the complete absence of, or disregard for, empathy, was the definition of inhuman? It disturbed me, terrified me, how easily it seemed to happen. I had interviewed so many refugees who had been not only raped, but raped in front of their children; whose children had not only been killed, but killed in front of them. It wasn't enough to kill the child, it had to be done in the way that caused the deepest distress and pain to their parents.

I asked Bereket, "How are you managing in Uganda?"

He nodded. "I have an Ethiopian friend who owns a restaurant. I stop by there every evening and he gives me the leftover food. I manage on this."

I told him, "I love Ethiopian food."

Bereket said, "Can I invite you?"

I smiled and looked away. I could not accept his invitation and didn't want to humiliate him by saying no. A look of realization – that, in spite of our banter, I could not accompany him to an Ethiopian restaurant, and never could – passed over his face, and he immediately looked embarrassed. I continued speaking quickly, to move past the moment, his humiliation; to patch over the gap between us – in power, in roles – that would never allow me to eat with him here.

I asked Bereket about his family and where they were, and he wrote the names out for me so that I could copy them into my notes. I misread the name of his sister, "Nehi," and noted that he had a sister called "Neil." Bereket spotted my mistake, pointed to it and laughed.

The interview took three hours. Everything Bereket told me correlated exactly with what he had told my colleagues in earlier interviews and with what we knew of the situation in Ethiopia and the government's actions, in the time before he fled. I read my notes one last time and looked up. "I will argue your case for resettlement to another country," I told him. "One where you can access medical care and counseling. I hope you can have a fresh start."

We signed the forms and I told him the office would contact him when there was a response. I moved my chair back as if to stand. Bereket stayed sitting with his hand on his plastic wallet. He spoke hesitatingly. "Can I show you some pictures?"

I said, "Of course."

He unbuttoned the folder and, not looking up, passed me the photographs. I looked at them, one by one. They were of his wife. She was beautiful, smiling. In one picture, she appeared to be sitting by a river. In another, they were together, his hand resting on her shoulder. In one, he was touching her hair. I said quietly, "I'm sorry."

Bereket sat the folder down and put his head in his hands. He said between tears, "I want her back."

I looked back at the pictures and said, "She was beautiful." I held the photos while Bereket cried and refugee children, their families awaiting interview, shouted and laughed, running up and down the hallway outside.

Bereket shook my hand before leaving, grasped it hard, his folder of photographs under his arm. I watched him as he left. This is what the torturers had left behind, a man, sick and heartbroken, who lived off scraps of leftover food. How would they feel, knowing this? Glad? Triumphant? I walked out to the courtyard and lit a cigarette. The children in the hallway had come outside and were still running, playing an indecipherable game. I made a silly face. I wanted, as always, to focus on this, the children's game, and convince myself that Bereket's experiences, the experiences all the refugees I worked with had fled from, were somehow unreal. The children giggled. I pretended I was going to run after them, and they ran, squealing with joy, pushing past each other, laughing, out of breath.

That afternoon, back at the office, I was assigned the case of a man from East Congo to review. His sister had been murdered and her remains dumped in a river. In his file were photos of his sister's body as they found it, in the water. I pulled them out and stared at them.

Ali walked into our office, smiling. He clasped his hands in front of his chest. "Working hard?"

I stood and threw the photos on the desk in front of him. I screamed, "People are fucking monsters!" and he stared at me, looking terrified, not knowing what to say.

Bionic Man

The psychiatrist rolled my file into a cylinder then let it unroll in her hands. She said, "In your case, I would suggest ECT." She paused. "Do you know what that is?"

I nodded noncommittally. She continued, "Electro-Convulsive Therapy. It's not as scary as it sounds." She waited for my response. I stayed silent.

"It has a good rate of success." She placed my file on her desk and lifted a notebook. "We can do it in Uganda. We would give you eight treatments, four weeks apart. You'd stay in hospital for the first sessions." She fingered the spirals of her notebook and said, "What do you think?"

I looked out the window. A man was kneeling beside the glass, watching me. He had a paintbrush in his hand. I asked the psychiatrist if she could ask him to leave.

She looked out. "He's just painting the balcony."

I nodded. "Can he do it another time?"

She stood up, pulled open the door and asked the man if he could come back. He shrugged, put aside his paint, and walked through the office to leave.

I asked, "Do you do it much?"

My psychiatrist looked confused.

I added, "ECT?"

She nodded, as though slowly recalling the thread. "It's quite a recent thing here, but we do perform it from time to time."

I said I didn't think I wanted to try it. My psychiatrist pulled a blank page out from her notebook. She said, "Have you considered Lithium?"

I told her another psychiatrist had suggested it, but I wasn't sure if I wanted to take it. My psychiatrist folded the blank page, then unfolded it again. She looked up. "What do *you* think would help?"

I looked at her then away. I put my hand up to my eyes. She nodded and said "'That's OK – it's OK to cry."

I looked out to the empty balcony and the abandoned pots of paint. I said, "I don't know."

By now, I was taking eight pills a day. Every time I saw the psychiatrist, she prescribed a new medication, each one to complement or counter the side-effects of the last. For the most part, I was still feeling despairing, self-loathing, consumed with guilt. My sleep was erratic and I was exhausted. The refugees' stories were becoming harder and harder to take.

I asked, "Don't you think I'm already taking too many drugs? Can't I at least give up one?"

The psychiatrist replied, "Which one?"

I suggested the mirtazapine, which was prescribed to make me sleep, and counter the effects of the sertraline, which left me wide awake all night. She said, "But you need that to sleep."

"But," I answered quickly, "the alprazolam helps with sleeping." The alprazolam was prescribed to complement the mirtazapine.

She nodded patiently. "Ok, but you still need the mirtazapine – to complement the sertraline." She looked around, as if trying to find a way to explain something obvious to someone inexplicably slow. "Imagine you are making a toy. Imagine you are making... Bionic Man."

I raised my eyebrows. She nodded slowly, having found the right analogy. "So you've made Bionic Man, but you have to add his legs. You add the left leg" – she held up a hand with one finger dangling – "And Bionic Man can get around by hopping." She made the finger hop. "But you add the second leg, and Bionic man can walk around properly." She added a second finger, and made them walk in the air. She smiled and I nodded at her logic. "Now, if you were to try to put the left leg in the right socket" – she bent one walking finger over the other – "it wouldn't go. The left leg wouldn't fit in the right socket. And the right wouldn't go in the left." She held both hands open in a gesture of "Ta-dah!" then paused, waiting for me to take it in. I looked at her blankly.

"So," she continued, "it's like that for you and these drugs – with one, you can hop around, but you need two to *really move*, and one won't fit in the other one's socket."

I looked to the strips of pills on the table, imagining one sprouting from each side of Bionic Man's trunk, and him hobbling freakishly around. I nodded, defeated. My psychiatrist looked pleased.

I told the psychiatrist about wanting to punch Peter, the refugee who had a tumor, and about throwing the photos in front of Ali and screaming at him. I told her about Michael, my boyfriend from Dublin. We had tried to keep up a long-distance relationship when I left, but we couldn't avoid the problems we had any longer, and split up. In the wake of the break-up, I had become more depressed, telling myself again, *He didn't want to commit to me because I'm a loser. I'm inadequate.* I told her how I tried to use my job to convince myself of my own worth. I'd keep count of the refugees I'd helped to resettle and tell myself, *These people's lives have changed because of my work.* But I didn't believe it was true. I continued to berate myself. *I'm not submitting as many cases as I should be. Anyone could do my job. In fact, more people would be submitted if someone else were in my role. I'm exhausted and distracted and working too slowly. There are families who could be resettled but are being left behind, and it's my fault. People will die because of my incompetence.*

My psychiatrist looked from me to the window and brought her pen to her mouth. "Maybe you just need a break? From work? From Uganda?"

I looked back to her and said "Maybe from work. I don't know."

She tapped the biro against her lips. "How long do you think would be appropriate?"

I looked around. I said, "I have no idea."

She asked, "A month? Two months?"

I answered, "A month."

She looked at me. She said, "I don't think a month is long enough. I'm going to recommend two months. So that you can have a break and see a doctor at home, who might be able to prescribe other drugs than what we have here." She pulled the lid from the pen and scribbled until the ink was coaxed out. She unfolded the page and began a letter. She asked for the name of my boss.

I looked at the page. I said, "I don't want him to know what's wrong with me."

The psychiatrist said, "I won't write any details. The letter will say merely that you're unwell."

I nodded and looked to the window again, then back to her and gave her Ali's name. When she'd finished writing the letter, she brought it to her secretary to type. She told me I would have to wait until it was done. I sat down in the corridor outside her office. I pressed the heels of my hands to my eyes, then looked up. The painter was sitting opposite and smiled. I looked at him for a moment, then told him I thought he could go back in. He thanked me, stood up, stretched, and knocked on the psychiatrist's door.

Mockingbird

The psychiatrist's letter recommending that I take leave for the vague "medical reasons" wasn't enough for our head office in Geneva, who requested a report with further information. I brought the original letter to Ali. He read it and looked at me with concern. I said, "I already sent this letter to Geneva, but they told me it wasn't enough."

Ali nodded sympathetically. He said, "My dear. Let me give you an example of how UN bureaucracy works. I had two months' sick leave this year. I was getting some work done to my teeth. Now look!" He brandished a sheaf of forms in front of him. They were photocopies of bills, some handwritten, some typed. I squinted to make out the heading on the first page. It said, *Porcelain veneers.*

Ali waved the papers. "I sent these invoices to Geneva to claim my money back. Do you know what they said?"

I peered at the total figure, printed to the right of the heading. *$8128.* I said, "No."

"They told me they wanted the original invoices! So now, along with the faxed copies, I have to send all the originals by pouch."

I looked at the bills, then at him. I shook my head to indicate something like outrage and despair. Ali said, "So I know how you feel. I'll do anything to help you."

He asked me what I needed. I said that Geneva wanted another report from my doctor and had sent a letter to the hospital telling her what they required, but that the doctor wouldn't get the letter as she wasn't going to the hospital for another week. Ali nodded his head slowly then raised his finger. He said, "So. What we'll do is - tomorrow, first thing, I'm going to send a driver to the hospital. That driver will pick up your letter. He will bring it to the UN clinic to be signed. Then he'll drive to your doctor's house, and instruct her that she must write a report as detailed in the letter." He paused. "Then the driver will leave. But I will have given the driver 2,000 shillings, and he'll have given that to your doctor. Then, when your doctor has written the report, she'll give the money to a motorbike taxi driver, and that driver will bring the report back to the UN clinic. I will personally call the UN clinic and tell them to fax the report to Geneva. Then by Friday morning – at the latest – we'll have a reply. What do you think?"

I stared at the stack of dentists' invoices, trying to process any of what he had said. I replied, "Well, I'm just wondering if my doctor will agree to give the report to a motorbike taxi driver... since it's confidential?"

Ali closed his eyes and nodded slowly as if taking this possibility in. He opened them again. He said, "She will put the report in an envelope and sign it at the seal."

I imagined the motorbike driver with the report tucked in his pocket, speeding toward the UN clinic. The report would blow away, or he'd open the envelope in case there was something better than 2,000 shillings in it, then disappointed, throw it in a ditch. I said, finally, "That sounds like a great plan."

Ali sighed. He said, "My dear, I don't want you to worry about this. I'm going to sort it out."

I thanked him and left the room. I returned to my office and sent Laura an email saying, "Did you see? He's wearing the pale green checked shirt with the dark green tartan pants."

Once, Laura had asked Ali where he'd bought the tartan pants. I'd bitten my lip while he narrated a long story of how he'd taken his mother shopping, and she proposed some things for him while he was there. He'd bought everything she'd suggested. This explained why all the new clothes – the checked shirts, shorts and pants, which he wore in combination, had appeared at the same time after he'd returned from sick leave. Laura wrote back, "I know! I saw it. It made my day."

I said, "I'll buy you a lunch if you can guess how much his teeth cost."

She replied, "$50,000?"

I didn't write back.

At lunch my colleagues were discussing UN pensions. Ali asked if anyone knew what would happen to his pension if he died, since he had no wife or children. Some colleagues told him that nothing would happen: the money would be kept by the UN.

"But is there no way," Ali asked, "I can arrange for it to go to someone else – like my niece?"

A finance officer, an Indian man called Arjun, said, "Not as far I know."

Laura spoke. "In any case, I've heard that the average UNHCR staff member is dead within three years of retiring."

Patricia, who had been listening intently to the conversation, leaned forward suddenly. "Why do you think that would be?"

Laura sat down the forkful of greens that she had been raising to her mouth. "Maybe because of the stress. Or because having to move country or continent every few years means you live lonely, work-filled lives. When you retire, you fall apart, because you have no family or friends, and no longer any work to occupy your time." She raised the greens again, and this time placed them in her mouth.

Another colleague, a Dutch woman called Hannah who had just returned from maternity leave, arrived with her four-month-old baby, and asked what we were talking about. Ali, who had been sitting in silence, not eating since Laura spoke, said, "Nothing." He stayed quiet for a moment, then stood up and took the baby's hand and shook it, and introduced himself. The baby smiled and gurgled back.

I left and called my doctor from the office. I told her of our scheme: the driver, the letter, the boda boda. She said she could pick up the letter from the hospital and deliver the report herself. I sent an email to Ali to tell him we didn't need his plan. I heard a baby crying suddenly and stood up and looked out my door. Ali was holding Hannah's baby, rocking her, walking her up and down the corridor, singing out of tune. Hannah was nowhere to be seen. I went back into the office. Ali was singing quietly, intently now, *Hush little baby, don't say a word, daddy's gonna buy you a mockingbird.*

The baby had stopped crying and started laughing. Ali sang, his accent heavier in his singing voice, "And if that mockingbird don't sing, daddy's gonna buy you a diamond ring."

The baby was laughing more and more noisily. I began an email to Laura, saying "Can you hear him?" then deleted it slowly, letter by letter. I shut the door and sat down again, staring at the screensaver: neon ribbons that appeared, and disappeared, in waves on my screen. I thought of Ali in his apartment, Judith cooking for him alone every night, and cleaning his apartment to his instructions. I thought of his stories about his young niece, whom he adored, but rarely saw. I thought of the money – over eight thousand dollars – he had billed the UN for porcelain veneers – when refugees didn't have enough money for food.

The baby was screaming with delight, laughing as though she'd been tickled. I tried to start writing again, but this time, I couldn't think of anything funny to say.

IV. Missing Out

Home

I called my mother, and told her I might be coming home. She said I should time my trip to coincide with a family reunion that was coming up. I said, "It's kind of... sick leave. I'm not sure I can request certain dates."

She responded, "Well, at least ask. Everyone will be there. But why are you coming on medical leave?"

I told her, "My doctor thought I should have a break."

My mother said, "It will look bad if you don't make the reunion. You should get leave for that date."

A week later, my approval for medical evacuation came through and I took a series of flights to Northern Ireland. The plan was to stay with my parents and receive treatment for depression – medication and therapy not available in Uganda – and, after some weeks, if I was better, to return to Kampala, and work.

The morning after arriving, I went to see a doctor in my parents' town. I explained why I was home and the psychiatric treatment I'd been having for the last couple of years. The doctor looked back at the UN medical clearance form she'd signed for me a year earlier. To the question of whether I'd ever seen a psychiatrist or taken any medication for mental illness, I'd written "No," fearing that the truth would prevent me from getting the job. I'd asked this doctor to sign the form as she didn't know me and had no access to my records, which, since they were in Dublin – the Republic of Ireland – were under another jurisdiction. The doctor, unknowing, had signed that I was mentally well.

She looked me over but didn't refer to the lie I'd asked her to sign off on. "What medication are you taking now?"

I listed all the drugs. The doctor raised her eyebrows. She said, "Are you sure you're on all of those? At the same time?"

I nodded.

She said, "Here... we would never prescribe all those drugs at once. At maximum levels?"

"Yes."

She continued, "Do you feel like life's worth living?"

I looked away. "I'm not going to do anything." I bit my finger and looked back at her. Once, in Uganda, a doctor had refused to let me leave his office until I promised I wasn't going to kill myself, "or do anything stupid like that."

She said, "How long does your depression date back?"

I looked to my lap. "Since I was fifteen, but it hasn't been all the time. This time, a couple of years."

She looked at the list of medications she'd noted. "Have you ever considered Lithium?"

I told her it had been suggested, but I'd said no.

She drummed her pen on the desk. "I'm going to refer you to the psychiatric hospital here. I'd prefer them to see you, given your history and all the medication you're currently on. Normally, it takes a while before you get to see someone, but... I can bypass the normal procedure and refer you directly. I will call the psychiatrist myself. You'll get a letter with the date of your appointment."

When I returned home, my mother told me she hadn't slept the previous night, worrying about my uncle – her brother. He had recently returned from the US to Ireland to attend rehab for alcoholism. He was refusing to go, and now he wasn't answering her calls. He was staying in the abandoned house of my late great-uncle. My mother said, "At least if he stays away, I won't have to worry about him."

I looked from the kitchen window. Our neighbor was cutting the hedge, but only on his side, so now it stepped up to ours. I stood up to make coffee. My mother asked, "How did it go with the doctor?"

I answered, "Ok. She made appointments with a psychiatrist."

My mother said, "Not too much milk in mine. Why?"

"I don't know, I guess she thought I needed it."

"Does she know who you are?"

I said I didn't know.

My mother said, "Well, at least this way you can tick the boxes – justify your medical leave."

I nodded and poured boiling water over the coffee grains.

I brought a coffee to my father, and he took it outside. There was a whirring in the distance, a lawnmower or an electric saw. My mother sat her coffee aside and filled a basin with soapy water. The dog had put her head on my lap. I played with her ears, trying to tuck them under her chin.

***

Two weeks later, my father drove me to see the psychiatrist. He told me he'd wait outside. He lifted a lever at the side of his seat to pull the seat back and closed his eyes.

The glass doors of the psychiatric clinic opened as I approached. I gave my name at reception, smiling as if to indicate *there's nothing really wrong with me.* The receptionist nodded and told me to sit down. There was one older couple there. The man tapped a rolled-up magazine on his knee. I smiled at the woman. She smiled, looking anxious, back. I wondered why they were here. Which of them had a problem? The woman was rubbing the man's back now. She must be the one supporting him. He was tapping the magazine faster, looking around. The receptionist leaned over the counter and called my name. The man threw the unfurling magazine on the table and stood up. His wife tugged at his sleeve but he pulled his arm from hers. He said loudly to the receptionist, "That's it. I've had enough. We've been here for almost an hour and everyone who comes in here after us gets called before we do."

The receptionist looked at him, then down to a large notebook on her desk. She said, "I'm sorry, you're here to see a different doctor. Your doctor isn't ready. She's with someone else."

The man asked her, still standing, "How long will it be?"

The receptionist turned back to the notebook. "I'm not sure... not too long now."

I looked apologetically to the man. The woman said, "We're not blaming you."

I smiled like I understood, then asked the receptionist where to go.

The psychiatrist spoke softly, and handed me a photocopied questionnaire to complete, similar to the questionnaire I had filled in several times before. She left the room while I ticked the boxes.

I feel that I am a guilty person who deserves to be punished:

Not at all
Just a little
Somewhat

Moderately
Quite a lot
Very much

I have had trouble falling asleep or staying asleep, or I have been sleeping too much:

Not at all
Just a little
Somewhat
Moderately
Quite a lot
Very much

I have felt bad about myself or felt like I am a failure or that I have let myself or my family down:

Not at all
Just a little
Somewhat
Moderately
Quite a lot
Very much

I have had trouble concentrating on things, like reading the newspaper or watching TV:

Not at all
Just a little
Somewhat
Moderately
Quite a lot
Very much

I have difficulty making decisions:

Not at all
Just a little

Somewhat
Moderately
Quite a lot
Very much

Very much, very much, very much, very much, very much.

I knew what my answers indicated. There was one series of questions, however, that always nudged my score slightly in the other direction.

I have lost interest in most (or all) of the things and activities that used to interest me:

Not at all.

I feel like I have nothing to look forward to:

Not at all.

I never lost interest in things that meant a lot to me. I never felt that I had nothing to look forward to. I was never not interested in traveling, or books, or the people I met. I never didn't look forward to more travel, or books, or meeting people.

The psychiatrist returned and took the questionnaire back, scanning it front and back. With a biro, she totaled the points and told me the score. She asked me if I knew what it meant. I nodded. She noted the list of medications I'd tried, and studied the list. She agreed that I could switch to a new antidepressant, one I'd read about and wanted to try. She asked me if I'd tried Lithium, or considered ECT. I looked at her. I gave her the same answers as I'd given the other doctors: I hadn't tried Lithium, I wasn't sure about ECT. I bit my lip. The psychiatrist tapped on her computer and the printer jerked on noisily. She pulled out pages of information on ECT and stapled them, and told me to read them and have a think. I folded them into my bag, thanked her and left.

Outside, I opened the car door, sat down and closed it. My father snored suddenly before turning and opening his eyes.

At home, my mother asked, "So how did it go earlier?"

I told her it had been OK. They'd done a test.

"What kind of test?"

I answered, "A questionnaire they use to assess levels of depression."

My mother was pushing the blinds aside to scrub the windowsill. I told her my score. She rinsed the cloth and wrung it out in the sink. She said, "If everyone did those tests, half the country would come out as having depression. It's just that they don't get asked."

Cure

The doctors' clinic in my parents' town had no receptionist. There was a touchpad computer screen with instructions to select the image of a man or woman. I touched the picture of the woman. The screen asked me to key in my date of birth. I tapped it in and it brought up my name and time of appointment and told me to have a seat. I sat on a vinyl-covered banquette opposite an elderly couple and a young woman holding a toddler, his face turned in to her shoulder. I lifted a magazine from the plastic table in the middle of the room. The cover had torn free from one staple and was hanging at an angle. Pink and yellow lettering was splashed across photographs of celebrities in bikinis. I flicked through the pages and the cover came off in my hand. A voice through the intercom called me to go to the consultation room. I dropped the magazine and cover onto the table and lifted my bag from the floor.

The doctor told me to sit while she looked through some papers on her desk. She asked me how I was. I said I was OK. She didn't look up. She pulled one paper from the pile, examined it and turned to the computer. She pressed a button then drummed her fingernails on the keyboard. She turned to me and frowned. "Did you see the psychiatrist?"

I said I had.

"How did it go?"

I told her the psychiatrist had written a letter, and pulled this from my bag. The flap of the envelope was sticking up from where I'd unsealed it to see what the letter said. The doctor pulled the letter out, unfolded it and read. She said, looking up, "So you got what you wanted."

I looked at her then away. She was referring to the new antidepressant that I had told her I wanted to try. She smiled quickly as though to say she was kidding, that she hadn't mean to suggest that it was all a sly ploy. She looked to the letter again then asked "Did the psychiatrist tell you to stop taking the other drugs first?"

"No."

She studied the letter.

I said, "She told me to come off the other drugs slowly while starting the new one at the same time."

The doctor folded the letter and turned to the computer. She typed slowly, then turned back to me and lifted the paper she'd pulled from the pile. She said, "There's something else. You remember the blood tests we did?"

I nodded. She smoothed the fold of the paper with her fingernail then tapped the paper against the desk. "They've shown that you have a deficiency of vitamin B12." I nodded again, waiting. She continued, "Do you know if you were tested for this before?"

I shook my head. She said, opening the paper, "I don't understand why this wasn't discovered earlier. How long have you been in psychiatric treatment?" I told her, this time around, two and a half years. She said, "Vitamin B12 deficiency is serious, and your levels are very low. A deficiency can result in neurological damage, and cause serious depression. It could be that for two years you've been taking antidepressants, when what you needed were vitamin shots."

I looked at her and waited. She said, "The deficiency of the vitamin is potentially the result of your body being unable to absorb it."

I asked her what this would mean. She said she was making an urgent referral to the hospital and I'd be called for tests. If these confirmed that I couldn't absorb the vitamin, I'd receive an intensive course of vitamin injections, then one every three months for the rest of my life. She told me I'd receive a letter with details of the hospital appointment, and wrote a prescription for the new drug.

Back at my parents' house, I looked up "Vitamin B12 deficiency, symptoms." I scanned the pages and read: *depression, insomnia, concentration problems, memory loss.* I skimmed down to "Treatment": "Deficiency can be easily treated by injections of Vitamin B12, six shots over twenty-four days, one shot every three months thereafter."

When my mother returned from work, I told her what the doctor had said. She said, "I'm relieved. But if what you need is the vitamin shots, why did she give you the prescription for a new antidepressant as well?"

I replied, "The shots won't start until I've had more tests. And maybe it's not that simple."

My mother said, "Vitamin B12 deficiency is pernicious anemia - an autoimmune disease. My aunt had it. Once you start with the shots, you won't need all the other drugs."

When my father came home, I told him about the results. He said, "Well, at least now you know what was wrong. That has to be good."

Later, I asked him if he could give me a lift to see my therapist. He looked at me. "Why do you have to still have to go there, now that they know what's wrong? When all you need is the vitamin shots?"

I shrugged. "My insurance covers the therapy. Maybe I should make use of that while I can."

He lifted his car keys from a hook above the phone and said, "Yes, but you don't need it now."

I pulled on my coat then pulled it off again. I told him, "I don't know what the shots will do. They might not work overnight."

My therapist asked me if I had any questions about our last session. I tried to remember what we'd discussed, but couldn't. I told her, "no."

She wrote my answer on a clipboard. She said she was going to do some exercises with me to help me feel differently about myself. I looked away. I wondered whether I should tell her, *Sorry, it's not that, I know now I'm just missing a vitamin.* Would she send me home if I did? I nodded and we began.

At home in the evening, I scrolled through my email, through the junk mail and work mail, until I found one message, and opened it and read it. It was from Michael, my ex-boyfriend in Dublin. When I'd finished, I sat and pressed my hands to my eyes. I read it again, then hit reply. I wrote, "I got my blood tests back today." I held my finger on the full stop until full stops filled the line. I deleted them one by one. I stared at the blinking cursor. Was there a way to make it stop? I closed my eyes. I wanted to say, *Guess what! Now I know why when you told me you loved me, I couldn't feel it.* I wanted to write *And there's a cure!* And believe it.

Making It

A few weeks later, my mother called my uncle, and this time got through. When she'd finished on the phone, she came into the kitchen, snapped on the kettle and sat down. She said my uncle had sounded despairing, desperate, hopeless. He told her that he'd been giving rehab some thought. He'd broken down and said that he'd resisted before because it represented his last chance. He didn't want to exhaust that hope, to lose it. Now, he said, he didn't have any choice. My mother told him she'd contact the rehab center and make arrangements for his admission.

I went to visit my uncle the day after he was admitted. The rehab unit was in the same hospital as the psychiatric clinic I attended. The reception faced a large room with chairs against all four walls. Two men were sitting close to the door, a chair between them, not reading, the television off. They looked up and said hello. The man closest to the door asked if I'd come to see someone. I gave him my uncle's name, and he said, "He's upstairs doing reflection."

A nurse walked down the hall and said, as a question, "Hello?"

I told her I had come to see my uncle. She smiled. "Ah. I'll tell him you're here. I'll just be a minute."

I stood by the door of the room and the men smiled at me and continued sitting in silence. The man furthest from the door said, "Not a bad day out there."

I nodded. He looked out the window. The other man continued to read. My uncle came down the stairs, tripping on the last two. He looked around then saw me. "Ah, sweetheart," he said, and held out his arms.

I hugged him and he rocked me side to side. The man who had commented on the weather looked up and smiled. My uncle told me to come outside so he could smoke. I asked if I could make coffee, and he pointed me to a kitchen.

The kitchen was tiny, with jars of teabags, instant coffee and sugar. There were packets of cookies, each wrapped up and labelled with the owner's name. I looked around for an electric kettle, but couldn't find one.

Then I saw, by a tray of identical upside-down cups, a tall geyser with paper taped above the tap, giving safety warnings. I made two cups of instant coffee, and brought them outside. My uncle was lying on a grassy bank just down from the building, tipping the ash from his cigarette into the grass. I lay beside him on my front, balancing the coffee on the level ground above us. I edged a cigarette out from his pack.

I turned to him. "How's it going?"

He shrugged. "It's exactly as I imagined it. Talking. Going into your head. Head-pickling." He pressed his cigarette out in the soil. "I don't have to talk for the first few days, just listen to the others. Next week I will have to talk, and that's what I'm dreading."

I asked him how it was scheduled. He told me, "9-9.30 – relaxation. Then group therapy. Lunch. A different kind of group therapy. Dinner, reflection, own time."

I blew out smoke and pushed myself up on my elbow, to better lift my coffee cup. "I had group therapy in Dublin before I moved to Uganda. When I started, I didn't think I'd be able to say anything. I was known as "the girl who doesn't talk." Then, after a few sessions, I felt like I was listening to these stories that other people were finding very hard to tell, but not giving anything back. I felt like I was eavesdropping. So I started to talk a little bit as well. And the other people were so supportive. In the end it helped me a lot."

My uncle nodded and lit another cigarette. "Yeah, maybe you're right. The other people are very nice. And I'm here now - I have to give it my best shot." He inhaled and raised his hand to shield his eyes from the setting sun. He blew the smoke out.

I asked, "Do you think it will help?"

He turned on his side to face me and inhaled again. I put my cigarette out and balanced the butt on blades of grass in front of me so I would remember to take it inside. My uncle said, "They say two out of every group of fourteen make it. Everyone I've met so far in my group is fucked. That has to make my chances of making it higher, don't you think?"

I turned to face him, and we stayed like that for a moment, laughing, then lay back and closed our eyes to the sun.

Missing Out

Shortly before I was due to return to Uganda, I walked through my parents' town to the pharmacy. It was drizzling, as it almost always was. My parents lived by the sea, and I took the path on the promenade, past people in rain coats, hoods up, hurriedly walking their dogs. At the pharmacy, I took the psychiatrist's latest prescription from my jeans pocket and unfolded it. I handed it to the pharmacist and waited by the counter. There was a poster on the wall opposite, advertising high-quality photo enlargements. It showed three different-sized photographs of a girl, a close-up of her face in a sun-hat, smiling, in front of an out-of-focus sea. The pharmacist came back to the counter with the boxes of tablets. She said, "Have you taken these before?"

"Yes."

She said, "It's a very high dose."

I told her, "I know."

She pursed her lips and nodded. She read out the instructions on the sticky label, *one every day with water, with or without food.*

I smiled in agreement and she put the packets in a white paper bag with the pharmacy's logo. I took the bag and left.

Back at my parents' house, I took a strip of pills from the box, and pushed one out with my thumb. I looked around and found a bottle of 7up, flat, and swallowed a mouthful with the tablet. I counted the rest of the tablets and climbed on a chair to put the boxes on top of a cupboard above the sink. I lay on the sofa and closed my eyes. Outside, it had started to rain. I walked upstairs to my old room – the room that had been mine as a teenager and was now, temporarily, again.

When I'd left Martha's house just over a year earlier, I'd brought my books and other possessions here to store them while I was in Uganda. I'd put some of my books on the shelves that were built into my bedroom wall. I knelt on the floor and pulled some of the books out from the lowest shelf. There were so many that I'd stacked them two-deep. Behind the outer layer were some that were turned with their spines to the wall. I was embarrassed and didn't want people – guests of my parents who might stay in the room – to see them. They were books about depression and insomnia – self-help books, and workbooks with exercises that I'd completed in pencil, until I'd lost hope in them, about a quarter-way through each book. I didn't know why I'd completed them in pencil – so that I could erase my answers and redo the exercises later to see if I'd improved? So that I could sell the books after they'd cured me? I pulled one of the books out. It was one that I'd used just before going to Uganda. There was a photo sticking out from just inside the front cover. I edged it out. It was a photo of Martha that her parents had given me – they had given the same photo to all of her friends. I sat on the floor against the bed, and stared at it. I had seen the photo before she died. In it, Martha was in a boat, kneeling at the front of it, holding the railings and looking back towards the person taking the photograph. She was laughing, tanned, her hair messed by the wind. The photo was taken while she was staying on a Greek island, on a holiday where people could choose from activities like yoga, and sailing, and art, and salsa dancing. The holiday had been free – she'd been offered it so that she could write about it in the paper where she was a features editor. I remembered her buying the clothes she was wearing in the photo – a white strappy tank top and long, tiered skirt. She come home with them, and shown them to me and another friend, and we'd teased her about her luck in getting junkets like this. She'd laughed and agreed, and joked about which of us she'd deign to bring on the next such trip. She'd already brought the other friend to a spa weekend at a five-star hotel, which she'd also scored on the basis that she'd write about it.

Martha had used the photo to accompany the article she later wrote about the holiday, in which she talked about how blissful it had been. The photo had been taken seven months before she died.

I climbed onto the bed, still holding the photo, and closed my eyes.

I thought of the questions in the depression questionnaire I'd done, the only ones that I could answer in a way that prevented me from having the highest – or worst – possible score.

I have lost interest in most (or all) of the things and activities that used to interest me: Not at all.

I feel like I have nothing to look forward to: Not at all.

Since Martha had died, every time I read a book I loved, I would think, *Martha will never read this book.* When I went to Uganda, and Rwanda, I thought, *She will never see these countries.* When I met people who inspired me, *She will never meet this person.* The idea that she was missing out on all of this was devastating to me. I felt guilty, and ashamed of myself, every day. At times, I wanted to put my cigarettes out on my arms. The stories I heard from refugees, and the treatment I saw them receive, filled me with despair. But I didn't want to die while there were still books, or places, or people out there that I loved, or could still love.

The following day, I emailed Geneva, and confirmed that I would be returning to Uganda the next week. I didn't feel cured, or even really better, but I had enough new medication and vials of B12 – even if I knew this was only a small part of what was wrong – to get me through another year. The break had left me feeling slightly less overwhelmed. I missed spending Saturdays barefoot in the garden, my back to the sun, my hands in the dirt. I missed drinking gin with Mario or Laura on my terrace. I missed the death-defying ride down the hill from my house on the back of a boda boda. I wanted to see some of the flowers I'd planted grow. I wanted to see some of the refugees I'd worked with finally leave for their resettlement countries.

I wanted to get back.

V. On The Run

On the Run

I returned to Kampala, to days interviewing refugees, and evenings drinking gin on the terrace, and weekends pulling up weeds in the garden. I took the high dose of the new medication, and asked the doctor in the office to inject the vials of B12 into me as per the prescription. I decided, restless one evening, to set up an online dating profile.

When I lived in Dublin, Martha had experimented with online dating. She had a dating column in a Sunday paper, and wrote humorous articles about these adventures and the men she met. She had recommended one site in particular, since it attracted, she said, men who were more left-wing, alternative, and intellectual. I decided to set up a profile there.

I provided the bare minimum of information – *I like smoking on my porch. I hate Comic Sans Serif font* – and uploaded a blurry photo that featured two-thirds of my face. I needed a username. I tapped the keyboard for a moment, then wrote *On the Run*. It fitted. I was on the run – from my depression, my feelings of inadequacy. The people I worked with were *really* on the run. It was a name that would intrigue men. Or repel them. Most likely repel. I pressed "Save."

I began looking through men's profiles. There were very few men registered in Uganda, and those who were, were very religious. I expanded my search to all English-speaking countries, including the US. I scrolled through the profiles. Some seemed nice. Over the next few days, a few contacted me to say that my hatred of Comic Sans Serif font made them sure I was their soulmate. We joked about this back and forth, before exhausting the number of messages I was allowed to send before having to pay to sign up. I liked them, but not enough to pay a subscription for a year.

Then I saw Judah's profile. In his description of himself, he had written "Usually strong, always kind." He had a kind face. And handsome. We began exchanging messages and I exhausted my limit with him too. I paid the subscription fee. We exchanged email addresses and wrote longer and longer emails, then began to talk on the phone. We Skyped. I began to leave parties early to call him. We spoke for seven hours at a time, the different time zones meaning that I was often speaking to him through the night.

On learning that I had struck up an online relationship – one I was hopeful about – with one of the first men I had communicated with, my colleague Rose raised her hands in apparent frustration. "You!" she exclaimed. "The rest of us are here, praying for a man, asking God every week at church to deliver, even *fasting* – and nothing. You do none of these things and yet," – she held her hand out as though presenting me with the head of John the Baptist – "you are handed this man on a silver platter."

I shrugged. "Rose, God helps those who help themselves."

Although I didn't like Rose's homophobia, and couldn't relate to her evangelical Christianity, and although we had, ultimately, very little in common, we had become friends. We shared an office across from Ali's bigger, corner office, and were forced, by this circumstance, to get along. I became fond of her and her sly sense of humor, though she would retract her jokes, panicking, if she thought they strayed into blasphemy. She went from regarding me with undisguised contempt, to tolerating me, to exhibiting some fondness for me too. We even made fun of each other now, and shared jokes and gossip about other colleagues, primarily Ali, our common enemy.

At thirty-five, Rose was a few years older than I. She complained regularly about the lack of men in her life, though she did nothing about this. She lived in a two-bedroom house that was overpriced, but since the organization that deployed her to the UN paid for it, she didn't care. She wore heavy navy polyester suits to work, regardless of the heat. She was beautiful, with high cheekbones and thick eyelashes. She changed her hairstyle – radically – every three weeks, though each elaborate new style – long braids, complicated twists – took, she said, eleven hours in the salon to create. She didn't normally leave the house, she told me, except to go to work, church, or the salon. Her housekeeper took care of trips to the supermarket, and cooked for her too. She was, however, learning to drive, though she was terrified of it. She had seen that in the UK, "L" plates – small white adhesive squares that clung to the windscreen – were used to warn others that the driver was a learner. These didn't exist in Uganda, but she wanted other drivers to know that she was still learning, and hence make allowances for her, so she made her own "L" plate – a giant white square of paper with a huge letter "L" drawn in red pen. She fixed this to the middle of her windscreen, thereby blocking most of her view of the road, and other cars. She was one of the few people I had ever met who was a worse driver than I.

I leaned across my desk to Rose. "I have an idea."

She sighed. "Do I want to hear it?"

"If you write up some cases for me," I told her, "You can take over my online profile. For free. I paid for it for a year, but I don't need it anymore."

Rose laughed loudly. "I'm not writing up your cases!"

I sat back. "Then the deal's off." I stared at my screen. I had in fact finished my cases for that day, it was Friday afternoon, and I was bored. Some of the staff had already gone home, but I was meeting a friend at 6pm, and it was now 5pm – too late to go home in between. I told Rose, "Fine. I'll give you my profile for free. Because I feel sorry for you."

Rose snorted. "What do I have to do?"

I typed in the name of the dating website, and logged in. My photo came up, the out-of-focus shot of me wearing wooden African beads and a sundress, on the porch in front of my house. I clicked on the "edit" button. I told Rose I needed a headline, just a few words that would sum her up. She thought for a few moments. "This is confidential?"

I told her she didn't have to use her real name. Only those on the site could see her profile, and they didn't have to know who she was, or where she lived. I said, "For every man you meet, you really do have to write up one of my cases."

She shrugged. "That part is fine, since I won't meet anyone. I will fill in the profile, but only to humor you." She closed some files on her desk and placed them in a drawer. "What kind of headline do you need?"

"A summary," I told her. "Like 'Loving but Lonely Nigerian.'"

"No," Rose said firmly, and as though she had thought of this before, " 'African Queen.' Now, what else do you need?"

I scrolled through the questions. " 'About me.' Describe yourself."

She thought for a moment. "Serious Christian lady – seeks serious Christian man. For a serious relationship."

I smirked. "That won't make them run away."

"Oh." Rose paused. "You think it's too much? Fine. Serious Christian woman – seeks Christian man. For a serious relationship."

I shook my head in mock exasperation. "Now we have to fill in your personal details. How would you describe your body type? Slim / petite, average, a little extra padding? Your hair length? Race?"

Rose grimaced. "Average. Long. Black." She opened a new file, then sat back. "Can I choose what I want from him? He must be a Christian."

I told her I thought that much would be clear. "Now we need more information. Your ideal way to spend a date?"

"In the park eating ice-cream." She hesitated. "No! Don't put that one. He'll just think I'm always eating junk food. Put something more exotic. 'On a beach in Zanzibar' – put that."

I nodded and typed up her answer, as though transcribing an interview with a refugee. "Ok. If someone gave you a million dollars right now, what would you do?"

Rose answered quickly. "I'd invest it."

I shook my head. "You can't write that. It should be interesting or exciting."

"But I would invest it."

"That's not," I insisted, "the point."

She sighed. "I'd go shopping in Paris." Then, "But really, I'd invest it."

I shook my head and scrolled down. "Where do you see yourself in twenty-five years' time?"

Rose answered without hesitating. "In serious real estate business."

I stopped typing and stared at her. "But what about all this humanitarian work?"

Rose winced. "I hope I'm not still doing that twenty-five years from now."

I sat back. "Really?"

Rose shook her head. "Of course not. This is just for now."

I wrote up her answer then stared at it. I had always imagined humanitarian work to be a vocation. I forgot that in many parts of the world, it was a pragmatic choice – there was more work, more money to be earned in the aid sector, than in other fields. In parts of Africa, the humanitarian sector, unlike other sections of the economy, was booming. In my human rights MA class, a woman from Egypt had said that many people she knew set up NGOs not because they cared about the proclaimed goals of the organization, but because they could use the NGO to obtain hefty international funding, and from this pay themselves a good salary. The UN already paid a good salary, and many people working for it – locals and internationals – were there for that reason only.

I looked again to the questions. "Five things you can't live without."

Rose switched off her computer and sat back. "Church, God, prayer, music, Christianity."

I shook my head and she ignored me. "Five albums you can't live without?"

Rose thought for a minute about this one. "Praise and worship. Christian jazz. Christian soul. Christian rap."

I noted this, then said, "That's only four."

Rose shrugged. "That's all I can think of."

I looked at the screen for a moment. "We'll pretend Praise and Worship are two different albums. Now – your favorite way to spend a weekend?"

"Jogging."

I looked up. "You jog?"

Rose shrugged. "Not yet. But I want him to think I'm fit."

I read on. "Last question. If you could be anywhere right now, where would you be?"

Rose thought for a moment. "Having a walk in the forest." She waved her hand, suddenly. "No, no, don't put that one. He'll think I'm just some kind of – African, living in the jungle."

I stopped typing and laughed. Rose laughed too. I told her, "We'll need a photo for your profile. Shall I take one with the camera we use for registering refugees?"

Rose looked aghast. "No! For that one, I need to go to the salon. You know, these things are very important. I need my hair to cover my forehead – and a pair of shades."

I shook my head. "Rose, they'll think you're a drug addict."

I read everything we'd written then entered "submit." I said, "If any men who saw my previous profile look at it now, they'll think I transformed overnight from a white, European atheist, to a black African evangelical Christian." I laughed and Rose began to laugh too. Our laughter was interrupted by a knock on the door. Ali's head appeared. He smiled at each of us in turn. "Working hard?"

I smiled back at him. "We're doing very important work."

Rose sniggered. Ali nodded. "Good, good. Because you two, the work you are doing, is helping very vulnerable people. They are depending on you."

Rose looked grave. "Yes."

Ali nodded again. "They don't have anyone else."

Rose looked to the floor. "Of course."

Ali gave a tight smile. "So keep it up." He left, and shut the door.

Rose and I were silent for a moment and I looked to the clock. I had ten more minutes before I needed to leave to meet my friend. I turned to her. "Are you thinking what I'm thinking?"

She lowered her voice to a whisper. "Do we have his picture?"

I nodded. "There's one on the system."

She smiled. "Well, then," she said, only half-joking, "He might be easier to work with if we succeed."

Titgate

While I was gone, Frieda and Claudia had finished their internships at the UN and left Uganda; Frieda to complete her master's, and Claudia to look for paid work. The sexual harassment incidents involving Mamadou, the deputy head of office, were rarely mentioned now. Mamadou continued to work at headquarters in Geneva. Linda moved to Geneva too, to serve out her remaining years at the UN in a high-level, but cushy post.

Ali left Uganda. While applying for new assignments, he was entitled to his salary – for two years – while not working. He assured us that he had apartments in both Washington DC and New York, and was looking forward to spending time there, and relaxing.

Godfrey, Ali's replacement, was a born-again Christian from Malawi. He instituted new policies soon after joining the office. Now, refugees weren't forbidden simply from being interviewed at the office, but from speaking to staff at the office at all, even at the compound gate. Having refugees loitering in front of the office would, Godfrey declared, would be unpleasant for the neighborhood, which was otherwise populated by embassies and diplomatic staff.

***

One morning, an email was sent to all staff, announcing that another anti-sexual-harassment training would be taking place in the office. It would be conducted by the human resources assistant. The training had taken place in UN offices all over the world and was, it seemed, unrelated to the events with Mamadou.

The day of the training was hotter than usual and the A/C was broken. The conference room was crowded and smelled of sweat. The discussions and role plays seemed to stretch interminably. The irony – that in a real situation of sexual harassment, no one cared – made it even harder to bear.

I sat next to Laura, and we amused ourselves with childish doodles on each other's notebook. I drew a stick figure with horizontal "X"s for eyes and a gun to her head. *This is how I feel.* Laura drew a figure with her tongue hanging out, a noose about her neck.

The HR assistant talked about forms of harassment in the office. Mostly they involved retaliation, like male managers refusing to write references for female staff who spurned their advances. A driver, sitting in the corner of the room with other drivers, raised his hand. The HR assistant nodded for him to speak.

"I feel like we," – he gestured to the other drivers – "are being harassed every day when female staff *know* they will have to ride in a Landcruiser, and step up high to get into it, and yet still wear short skirts." He shot a sly glance at a group of female junior international staff at the back of the room. The other drivers nodded in vigorous agreement.

The HR assistant looked uncomfortable. She brought her hand to her chin. "Yes, that *could* be seen as a form of harassment, if these staff were *deliberately*" – she searched for the right word – "flaunting themselves." She paused, her cheeks reddening. "But perhaps," her voiced trailed off, "they are not?"

The driver folded his arms, his expression dissatisfied. The HR assistant cast about the room, and spotting another raised hand, quickly called upon the questioner to speak. It was a Ugandan man who worked in finance. He looked troubled.

"Sometimes when I shower in the morning, my two-year-old son walks in, and sees me naked. Am I harassing him by letting this happen?"

The HR assistant's cheeks reddened still further. "No, no, you aren't harassing him. He is only young. He's your son. It is not inappropriate."

Laura turned to me and, chin down, surreptitiously drew her finger across her neck, making the gesture for slitting her throat.

"We needed this training before *Titgate*," she said.

I giggled. She had never referred to the incidents this way before. She had not been there when they had happened, and only heard of them through me, the interns, and occasional gossip.

I looked around the room. No managers had come to the training. The room was full of junior staff, who were mostly women. Most of those who needed the training weren't even there.

Our sketches of guns and nooses and references to *Titgate* – all of our twisted jokes – made everything easier to bear. Humor was our only remaining defense.

Soon after the anti-harassment training, Sofia, a representative from the department charged with investigations, arrived from Geneva. She had come, I only learned afterwards, to investigate bullying allegations against a senior staff member in another department. The details of the allegations, since they were confidential, were hazy, and not necessarily reliable.

Sofia set up office in the building, to spend a week and a half interviewing everyone there. She called us individually to meet with her, not specifying what she was investigating, opening only with, "How are things at work?"

Five minutes into the interview, I began, "Ever since the sexual harassment incidents with Mamadou," and Sofia stopped typing, lowered the screen of her laptop and looked up.

"Which sexual harassment incidents?"

I explained, "The incidents from last summer."

She shook her head. "I don't know what you mean."

I looked around. The door was shut, the window too. The fan was ruffling a stack of papers on a bookcase, creating a muffle of white noise. "Is this confidential?"

Sofia nodded, her expression slightly exasperated. "Of course."

I told her everything that had happened with Mamadou, and she typed urgently, focused, as I spoke. After another five minutes, she looked up. "We will have to resume this on Monday." She consulted her calendar. "Can you come at ten o' clock?"

At Monday's interview, Sofia took email addresses for Claudia and Frieda, and told me she would need to contact them too. Her mission, I learned, had been extended by two days. I wondered if it was to investigate this further. Sofia assured me that the people involved would not know that I was the one who had brought this up with her, and I would be protected from retaliation.

Before I left, Sofia asked why I had not reported Mamadou's actions to her office earlier.

"Linda advised us against it," I told her, as though it was obvious. "She said everyone in the office would be interviewed and would come to learn of what had happened, and we would be humiliated, ashamed. Then of course," I added, "Ali told Frieda that if she did report the events, she would never work for the UN again."

Sofia didn't speak, only nodded, and blinked hard. She exhaled loudly, causing the papers on her desk that were already fluttering in the breeze of the fan, to levitate an inch or two completely, then drop. She began, again, to write.

Leaving her office, I felt regretful. Why hadn't I pushed for an investigation back when the events took place? Was it this simple? Linda had told us that a mission from the inspector general's department would be complicated, humiliating, huge. But was this all that would have taken place? We could have – it now seemed possible – stopped Mamadou from being promoted and transferred to another office where he could act the same way. Why had I fallen for what Linda had wanted us to believe? Why hadn't I requested the investigation alone, or tried to persuade Frieda and Claudia that it was the right thing to do?

But now at least, perhaps something would be done. I felt satisfied – smug, almost – to think of Linda discovering that the investigation had been launched, a year and a half later, when she would have been certain that the affair was long over with, successfully dealt with, covered up. I looked forward to hearing what would happen; to seeing justice finally being done.

Gift

Celestin, my gay Burundian client, was rejected for resettlement by Denmark. I spoke to the interpreter from the interview with the Danes and he told me that Celestin, nervous, had given an inconsistent and muddled version of his reasons for fleeing Burundi. If he couldn't prove that he was a refugee – that he had a well-founded fear of persecution in Burundi – his situation in Uganda wasn't even relevant. I arranged to meet him to get more information to try to strengthen his case.

At the NGO's office, I almost didn't recognize Celestin. His hair was styled in chin-length braids, secured by brightly colored beads. He smiled and greeted me as "*tantine*" – auntie.

"Thank you for the money," he said shyly, "I had my hair styled." He touched his hair and I noticed that his nails were painted tangerine. I bit my lip to hide my bemusement. He had received $40 after months of barely being able to eat, and had spent the money on a new hairstyle and orange nails? I guessed that he had chosen morale over food. But I didn't understand how, knowing the risks, he was willing to walk around with a hairstyle that was usually, in Uganda, worn by women, and painted nails. Or was I, like Rose, assuming he had a choice in how he appeared and behaved?

I told him that Denmark had rejected him, and he nodded, pushed a stray braid behind his ear, then said in French, "Thank you for trying."

I assured him we would submit his case to another country, and asked him to contact me if he had problems. He thanked me, then stood, smoothing his braids down once more, and left.

Upon arriving at the NGO's offices weeks later, I bumped into Miriam, the counselor. She asked me to come into her room. I sat down, and she waited for the NGO's director, who was hovering by the door, to leave.

She spoke quietly, looking up periodically to the window in her door to make sure no one was outside. "I wanted to talk to you about Celestin."

I nodded. Since I had last seen him, Celestin had been rejected by two more countries. The interpreter had told me that, again, he hadn't appeared credible in his interviews: he had been nervous, refusing to make eye contact, giving inconsistent versions of his reasons for flight. Even so, I wondered if I had failed to make his case convincingly enough. How could resettlement countries not see that he needed to leave, that he wasn't safe here?

"He has had some problems," Miriam told me. "He's been arrested five times now, and beaten – badly – every time."

I stared at her. "Arrested for what?"

Miriam looked to the door again. "Because of his appearance. The police see him and assume he's homosexual. They arrest him and beat him to teach him a lesson. But still," she sighed, "he doesn't learn. He continues to dress –" she hesitated, "the way he does."

I hadn't known about any of the arrests. For a moment, I wondered why Celestin hadn't told us, then realized that I wasn't even sure he had a phone. I had always arranged interviews with him by posting a message on the noticeboard on the wall of the NGO' s building. This is how we scheduled interviews with refugees who didn't have cell phones: we posted a note with the name, time and day of the scheduled meeting, and expected that another refugee who had seen the message would find them and tell them when to come. No one ever missed an appointment. Often, refugees were so desperate to be resettled out of Uganda that they would stop by the NGO's premises every day, just to see if their name had finally been added to the list.

Celestin could have come to our office to tell me about the arrests, but the police at the gate would have turned him away. He had no reliable way of reaching us to tell us he'd been arrested and beaten. Even if he had: what could we do? We couldn't guarantee his protection in Uganda, and some staff didn't even believe he deserved to be protected. In my role, I could try to persuade another country to accept him, but so far, I hadn't even been able to do that.

I returned to the office and re-read the argument I had made on his behalf. I added the details about his arrests and upgraded the status of his case to urgent. I contacted our regional office in Kenya, and they told me they would submit the case to Canada, but that even if he was accepted, it wasn't guaranteed he would be able to leave soon.

***

A year after I had first met him, Celestin was still awaiting interview by Canada. No one had seen him in months. I still had no openly gay clients, though I had several male clients who had been raped by the priests who had taken them in. One of these priests was known in the international community for providing refugees with food and a place to sleep. It was assumed that he did this for Christian reasons. No one seemed to know – or perhaps care – that he was raping the young male refugees, who had nowhere to turn for protection. Many of the refugees didn't speak English or any local language, and would receive no help from the police. The refugees who told me about the priest's actions begged me not to report him to the police, for fear of retaliation. I had met the priest at a party given by an ambassador and he had smiled and held out his hand, his manner obsequious. I recognized his name and held onto his hand and met his eye long enough that a shadow passed over his face, realizing there was something wrong. When I mentioned that I worked with refugees, including many who had been abused, his face grew paler and his smile tighter. He wriggled his hand out from my grasp, looked at his watch, and quickly left.

***

On a Sunday afternoon in late 2007, I was reading in front my house, when Mario appeared. I hadn't seen him in weeks. We hugged, and I asked him if he wanted a drink.

He shook his head. "No. I just wanted to know if you wanted to come out later. I'm going to a gay club." He raised his eyebrows. "What do you think?"

I thought for a moment. "I have to work tomorrow."

Mario rolled his eyes. "It's a gay club in Uganda! Come on!"

I laughed. "What time?"

He told me he would pick me up at eight.

It was almost seven. I ran a bath and squeezed in a few drops of vanilla *Fa* – the only shower gel available at the local supermarket. I opened a bottle of Kenyan Tusker beer and got in. The bath was only one-quarter-full – our water was now being switched off regularly, and I was afraid to use too much. I switched on the tiny battery-operated radio by the side of the bath. It was tuned to the World Service and broadcasting *World Have Your Say*. I sipped the beer and lay back, closing my eyes.

Half an hour later, I stood, wrapped in a towel, in front of the closet. What did I wear to a gay club in Uganda? My closet held a rail of dresses, all handmade by my tailor, and ironed neatly by Dorothy. I picked one out. It was made from a kanga that I'd bought on the beach in Zanzibar. A friend who'd visited the UK had brought back a copy of Vogue, and from that I'd cut out an image of a dress that I liked. The tailor had reproduced the dress almost exactly with the kanga. It came just above the knees, had no sleeves, just straps, and a narrow belt made from the same fabric. The Vogue design it was based on was a Prada, and so I called it my Prada dress. With the fabric and tailoring, it had cost twelve dollars. I pulled it on and slipped my feet into beaded leather flip-flops I'd bought at the market.

When Mario came back to collect me, he exclaimed when I walked out. "The Prada dress! Hoping to meet someone? I don't think you'll have much luck."

I smiled and said, "Maybe I'll meet a man who got lost and ended up there by mistake?" The truth was I was still communicating nightly with Judah, and had fallen for him, and was hoping we could eventually meet.

Mario shrugged. "Actually, you might. The club's not actually in a gay bar – those don't exist, obviously. It's a gay night in Zodiac, a regular bar."

I locked the patio doors that opened onto the porch and then, when we'd stepped out into the garden, the metal grille that covered the porch. "Sundays are gay nights?"

Mario laughed. "They can't be so open. It doesn't work like that. The time and location of a "gay night" is chosen maybe a week in advance, then word is spread in the community. A friend texted me a week ago to say there'd be one tonight in Zodiac. The owners of Zodiac don't know about it, and neither will half of the people going there. But I wanted to invite you – you said you wanted to come."

It was true: I had told Mario that I wanted to go to a gay club. I was curious – in a country where gay people were hunted down and physically attacked, how could a gay club even exist? Who would be willing to go there? What would it look like?

Downtown was busy with matatus – minibus taxis – honking, crowds of people on foot, and marabou storks picking at rubbish on the side of the road. We wove our way through the traffic, taking wrong turns as Mario tried to remember where the club was. He called out of the window of his car for directions, and people pointed, bemused, and tried to explain.

When we found the bar, Mario parked, and paid the men whose self-appointed role was to "protect" the cars along that stretch of the street.

The club was in a brick shack, with tin roof. The word "Zodiac," an image of a man and woman dancing, and the zodiac signs, were painted crudely on the side. In the front part of the room, men and women sat on folding metal chairs in front of a stage. A woman in halter-neck top and shorts, sang, with bored-looking backing-singers behind her. The audience sipped from bottles of Fanta, occasionally a beer, and watched them. A few groups of men, also sipping Fanta, stood watching from behind the chairs.

"Those are the regular customers," Mario whispered. "They're just here for that show. They don't know that a gay night is taking place here tonight."

We walked through the crowd to the bar at the back of the room. A few people looked up – we were the only white people as far as I could see – and then turned back to the performance.

The back of the room held an entirely separate crowd. I looked around. People were huddled, laughing. Two men were on a table dancing. A woman approached me and told me she liked my dress. I turned to Mario. "Is she flirting?"

He laughed. "Of course!"

We ordered local Bell lagers and a man in traditional tribal costume – sleeveless shirt, long beads and checked sarong – greeted Mario with a kiss on the cheek. Mario introduced me. "This is Karamojong John. Of course, that's not really his name – he's just John – but he's from the Karamojong tribe, and we have to find a way to distinguish him from all the other Johns."

John held out his hand, laughing. "I am Karamojong John! But you can call me 'KJ'!" He laughed. "Pleased to meet you!"

When we'd finished our introductions, he moved into the group to dance.

I was surprised but wasn't sure why. Why wouldn't there be gay men in a traditional tribe like the Karamojong too?

I finished the beer, lit a cigarette and joined Mario dancing. The crowd at the back had grown raucous – more men, and one woman, were dancing on the tables now. The audience for the show at the front of the room continued to appear oblivious or indifferent.

After a while, Mario and I left the crowd and made our way to the bar to buy more beer. We stood sweating, clutching the bottles of Bell. They dripped with condensation. I rubbed the label of mine, and it slid down the side of the bottle. When he had recovered his breath, Mario nudged me and whispered, "I'm not sure about that guy over there."

I squinted at the man he was gesturing toward. He stood alone, leaning against a table, holding a Coke that he wasn't drinking.

Mario continued, "He's probably an infiltrator."

I sat my Bell on the bar and turned to him. "What do you mean?"

Mario shrugged. "There are always infiltrators at gay nights. They pretend to be gay in order to find information about when and where gay clubs are taking place, then blackmail people not to inform on them to their employer, or the police."

"How do the infiltrators know where people work?" I asked.

Mario sipped on his beer. "They make a point of following the people who come here, and finding out everything about them." He paused. "I'm just surprised I haven't been approached yet. But," he took another drink, "because I'm white, I won't be arrested."

I raised my eyebrows and asked, "Why not?" though I knew the answer.

"Too much media attention, too much trouble. I could lose my job, but I don't think they'd risk arresting and beating me."

I looked at the suspected infiltrator. He was still sitting against the table, watching, still not drinking his Coke. I thought about Celestin. He had no one to protest if he was arrested and beaten. He couldn't afford a bribe. Unlike Western expats, he couldn't rely on any media outcry if he was attacked in Uganda simply for appearing to be gay. Unlike most Ugandans, he had no family or community of friends here to intervene, if they didn't support his persecution. The Ugandan government wouldn't go to great lengths to protect a Burundian national even if he wasn't gay, and the Burundian government couldn't – and wouldn't – protect someone who had fled from the country, and possibly opposed them. Our organization was mandated to protect people like him, but since many staff refused to work with anyone who was homosexual, and felt that his persecution was his own fault, he was left to himself. He was as vulnerable as it was possible to be.

I looked around. There were even more people dancing than before. One of the tables shook: it was flimsy, plastic, barely able to sustain the weight of the four men who were dancing on it now. I didn't understand the bravery of anyone here. They risked losing their jobs and being arrested and beaten, by not hiding who they were. I had imagined the club to be discreet: impossible for an outsider to know it was even gay. Instead, it was how I pictured a gay club to be in, I didn't know, San Francisco in the seventies. It was riotous, uninhibited, celebratory. I was convinced that, in the place of anyone here, I would not be nearly so courageous.

***

In early 2008, I received word that Celestin had been accepted, finally, for resettlement to Canada. There were various hurdles to complete before he could leave: medical and security checks, and pre-departure orientations, so he would know what to expect when he arrived. Months passed while these took place. In May 2008, Celestin showed up at the office gate. A guard called me in my office, asking, in accordance with Godfrey's policy of not speaking to refugees at the office at all, if he should tell him to leave. I looked at Rose, sitting across from me. She was typing, but I knew she was listening to the call. "No," I told the guard. "I'll be straight down."

Celestin was standing with a friend who had come, he said, to interpret. He was clutching a package wrapped in plain white printer paper. He handed it to me, along with a piece of graph paper folded in four into a square. I looked from him to his friend. The friend spoke.

"Celestin wanted to bring you this present to thank you for everything you've done for him."

I took the present and looked around. The guard was watching me closely. Accepting gifts from refugees was forbidden, in case they were used as bribery in return for resettlement. This was different though, I reasoned, as Celestin had already been accepted for resettlement. There was nothing he could bribe me for: his case was with the Canadian authorities now, and I no longer played any part.

I opened the package, while Celestin watched, smiling, biting his fingernails, which were now painted a shimmery pink. Inside was a tailor-made outfit: a shirt and skirt made in an African fabric, pale blue with a pattern of roosters. I pulled the outfit out and held it up.

"I didn't know your measurements," Celestin said shyly. "But I thought you were about my size, so I asked the tailor to fit the clothes on me."

I smiled, imagining a local tailor fitting the skirt, and the frilled top, on a man. I thanked Celestin, held the clothes against my body, agreed that we must indeed be the same size, then leaned forward and kissed him on the cheek. He blushed, but looked proud. I could see, from the corner of my eye, the guard bristle. I ignored him, and opened the square of graph paper. Celestin had written on it, in neat cursive:

"Merci encore pour tout ce que vous avez fait pour moi, ma vie a changé depuis que je vous ai vue, vous m'avez empechée les chagrins et les soucis."

Thank you again for everything you have done for me, my life has changed since I met you, you have saved me from sorrows and worries.

I felt a tightening inside me. I had done only what was required of my job, a job for which I was, by local standards, well paid. I had submitted him for resettlement, but hadn't been able to protect him from the arrests and beatings. I didn't feel deserving of this gratitude.

I thanked him again. I wished him luck with his move to Canada, folded the white paper around the present again, and made my way back to the office.

As I entered my office, Rose pushed away her keyboard and sat up. She looked at the package under my arm, then at me. "What is it?"

I stuffed the graph paper note into my pocket, then pulled the wrapping off the present. "It's an outfit." I held it up.

"Who for?" she asked, as though there could be any doubt.

I smiled. "For me."

Rose said nothing, then "From whom?"

"Celestin," I told her, then smiling, "Do you think it will look good on me?"

Rose shook her head. "You can't accept gifts from refugees."

I nodded, laying the outfit out on my desk. "I understand. But Celestin has already been accepted for resettlement, so I don't technically have any part in his case anymore."

She said, "I'm not sure if that makes any difference. The appearance is still the same. Other refugees who see you accepting a gift from him wouldn't know that, and could accuse you of accepting a bribe."

"But no one saw us," I argued, wondering if she had noticed Celestin's friend, who had been with him the whole time.

Rose stood and lifted some files from her desk. "It's the rule. You should give the outfit back."

She leaned forward to switch off her computer, then left the room. I looked again at the outfit. I pictured myself decked out in the roosters, and smiled. The top and skirt together might be a little much, but I could wear the top with jeans. How could I have rejected the outfit without offending Celestin? Wouldn't it be insulting to him to imply that I couldn't accept his present because it would be assumed to be a bribe?

I wondered if Rose would report my acceptance of the gift to anyone. Could I lose my job for breaking this rule? I looked at the clothes once more. I pictured Celestin picking out the fabric, having it measured on him, wrapping the finished outfit carefully in the printer paper. I thought about the guard not wanting to allow him in through the gate, about the look of disdain he gave him as he did. I thought about Godfrey's policy of not allowing refugees to enter the premises at all. I looked down at the outfit. I would keep it. I couldn't give it back to Celestin. I would even, I resolved then, wear it to the office – I would sit across from Rose, decked out head-to-toe in blue roosters, as a rebuke.

***

By mid 2008, Celestin still hadn't departed for Canada. His acceptance hadn't been finalized. A month before I was due to leave the country, I saw him at the NGO's offices. He was almost unrecognizable: his face swollen and purple, one of his eyes shut, and his lip cut open. I gasped when I saw him. I took him aside, called over an interpreter, and asked what had happened.

"The police," he said, "beat me."

I asked how many times he had been arrested now. He brought his hand to his mouth. His pale blue nail polish was chipped. He wore black eyeliner, unevenly drawn. He looked down. "Thirteen."

I was shocked. I felt a stab of shame. How was Celestin still being arrested and beaten up like this? How had we failed so badly to protect him? Patricia had left now, and there were very few colleagues remaining who did not oppose those who were gay. Godfrey still prevented refugees from coming to the office at all. Though Celestin had been provisionally accepted for resettlement to Canada, he had now been arrested and beaten thirteen times in the time it was taking to leave.

As outsiders, we couldn't intervene with the Ugandan police, but I wondered, still, if there wasn't anything else we could have done. Celestin had nowhere else to turn. I wondered too if I couldn't have tried harder to stand up to Godfrey, so that Celestin could at least have come to us for help. I had tried, once, to stand up to him, over something else, and as a result he hadn't spoken to me for months. After this, I hadn't challenged him again.

I told Celestin that I was leaving Uganda, and he looked up, biting his lip. "But what if I am not accepted, if I have to remain here?"

I said, "You should be accepted. It's just taking some time. But I will assign someone to take over your file, just in case." I said this, though I had no idea who this would be. Laura would be willing to take him on, but she was leaving soon too.

I shook Celestin's hand and told him, unable to think of anything else to say, "bon courage." *Good luck.*

What to Believe

Dorothy got engaged not long before I left Uganda. Her fiancé was a geography teacher. I realized that Dorothy's combined earnings from me and her other clients would probably be more than her fiancé's as a teacher at a secondary school. Joyce, I was certain, earned more than the school's principal. Cleaning the houses of expats – especially UN expats – could be more lucrative than teaching local children.

I had seen that rich Africans and Indians treated their housekeepers as unfairly as white expats did. The only difference, it seemed, was that white expats experienced more guilt, or at least talked about their guilt more. But the guilt was meaningless: when it didn't change actions, as it usually didn't, it helped no one. It was a useless emotion: worse than useless, since those who experienced it confused it *with* action. I, and many of the other white expats I had met, believed, somehow, that as long as we felt guilty, as long as we felt bad about the inequality we saw, it was OK. We expressed contempt for the rich Africans and Indians who, unlike us, seemed to have no problems with how their staff lived.

We were often reassured by our guilt – it set us apart from what we saw as the more unscrupulous of the Indian and African employers – but we still tried to assuage it. We made excuses not to pay our housekeepers more, arguing, *It will mess with the local economy.* We bargained down prices on locally-made crafts, saying, *It will bump up prices and make crafts unaffordable to locals* – knowing that this wasn't actually true, that some expats paying a few dollars more for a handmade bag or beaded necklace would have no effect other than to help those who had made them earn a little more.

Expats who worked in community development, who campaigned for locals to earn fairer prices for their goods, still bargained prices down to below that which was fair, and then bragged about it, scoffing at those who paid more.

Local people's needs were also, the ugly subtext went, *less than ours.* Why else did refugees on UN financial assistance receive less than one hundredth of what UN staff were given?

We chose what to believe in order to feel better about ourselves.

Dorothy helped me clean up and pack before I left, and carried my cases on her head to the taxi on the day that I went to the airport. Before getting into the taxi, I thanked her and wished her good luck. She shook my hand solemnly. Then I gave her a tip of forty dollars, the equivalent – I had felt ashamed, but tried to tell myself that *wasn't it above average wages?* – of what I had been paying her per month.

Alhamdulillah

A year and a half after I submitted an application for Ayaan, my Somali client who was working as a sex-worker, to the authorities, the American Embassy added her to a list of people they would interview and decide whether to accept or reject. They called me and then Ayaan, to inform us of the next steps.

Some weeks later in the office, a colleague told me that Ayaan was outside, arguing with the police at the gate. I found her with two young boys holding either hand. I looked at each of the children. The smaller boy wriggled, smiled shyly, then pulled a fold of Ayaan's dress across his face. I said, "Ayaan, is this Abdullahi?"

She looked at the boy and nodded, smiling.

I said, "Abdullahi! What a gorgeous boy. And you've gotten so big."

Abdullahi looked out from behind Ayaan's dress, giggled, then hid again. He was beautiful, with long eyelashes, dimples and a mischievous smile. His brother was tall with lighter skin and deep-set, serious eyes. He held out his hand to shake mine.

A policeman continued watching us, one hand holding the gate open, the other clutching his rifle by his side. I told him, "It's OK, she's with me."

He shook his head. "Refugees can't come into the compound."

I looked at Ayaan and sighed, and we moved to the other side of the gate.

Ayaan spoke in a frenzy, looking away when tears came to her eyes. She said, "I've come to see you many times, but they won't let me through the gate."

"I know," I told her, "It's the office policy."

Godfrey had continued to warn us that refugees loitering by the gate would cause complaints from the neighbors, the embassy staff nearby, and the office would be forced to relocate as a result. No one wanted our office to have to move, since its location in a pleasant diplomatic neighborhood meant staff could live there too, and have a short commute – to and from work and home for lunch. It seemed logical that the office, like local NGOs, should be in the areas where refugees lived. But these areas were slums, far from where UN staff resided. Besides, only a small number of staff actually met with refugees; many had never spoken to a refugee at all.

I told Ayaan, "The guards won't even call me at my desk anymore to tell me that you're here. I only knew because a colleague saw you at the gate."

Ayaan asked, "But where do we go if we need help?"

I looked around. The policeman was still watching us from behind the rails. "I don't know, Ayaan."

She stared at me. "But isn't that what you are being paid to do? I mean, this organization?"

I nodded, looking away. I was embarrassed, and wanted to dissociate myself. I wondered about my contribution to the problem. When Godfrey had announced that refugees could no longer come to the office, I hadn't said anything, hadn't objected to the policy. I had learned to expect only retaliation; I had seen how those who had challenged Godfrey, and other senior managers' authority, had suffered. They were treated with contempt, given bad references, lost their jobs. I had previously challenged smaller things, and learned that the only outcome was that I would be punished. Now, worn down, I stayed quiet.

Ayaan continued, "You are the only one who has ever helped me."

I said, "Ayaan, I didn't know you had come to see me so many times. The police have been instructed not to let refugees in. We've been told to give refugees appointments to meet us in the NGO's office, on our terms."

I looked back to the policeman, still watching us. I said, "I'm sorry. That's what we've been told. That's why I never knew you were here."

Ayaan pulled her boys closer to her. "What you did before – arranging that money, giving us a chance to find a home in the US – my sister, you helped us."

I said, quietly, "No, that was my job. That's what I get paid to do."

Ayaan shook her head, then said, "But the reason I needed to see you –"

She looked around, then moved further from the gate. Almost inaudibly, she told me, "The American Embassy have called me for medical tests – to see if I'm in good health."

I nodded. "That's normal."

Ayaan continued, "Yes. But what if they find that I'm not? Will they refuse to take me then?"

I was confused. "Are you unwell?"

The older boy was holding his hand out to me again, and I took it. He smiled solemnly, and I shook it. I looked to Ayaan. I understood, suddenly, and without doubt.

"Do you mean – ?"

Ayaan nodded and looked away. "I had no choice but to do that work."

I paused then said, "As far as I know, Australia is the only country that refuses to take people because they are HIV positive. The US – it should be OK."

Ayaan sighed and said, "I'm so glad."

I bit my lip and looked to the boys. "And Abdullahi?"

She touched his hair and nodded.

"Yusuf?"

She shook her head, "No."

I looked around. I wondered if this could have been prevented. If Ayaan had been able to approach our office – which had a large budget for precisely this purpose – to tell us that she had financial difficulties, she might have been able to avoid the sex work that had apparently caused her, and then her son, to be HIV positive. Godfrey, with his refusal to allow refugees to approach the office, bore huge responsibility for their situation, and my, and other staff's, inability to stand up to him was implicated too. Further, if we gave refugees more financial assistance and paid ourselves less, Ayaan's situation might have been mitigated. I felt sick to think of these possibilities: that our cowardice and greed were part of the reason Ayaan and her son were ill.

I told Ayaan, "If you are accepted by the US, I hope you will get good medical care."

She looked down to her sons, who were squirming now to let go of her hands. "When will I know?"

I said, "You'll have the medical tests, then the interviews, then an answer a few months later. If they accept you, you'd be leaving maybe three months after that. Six or seven months from now."

Ayaan asked, "What are our chances?"

I said, "I really don't know. I argued your case, but only the US can make the decision now."

She nodded. "Thank you."

She let the boys go and they ran, chasing each other in circles, laughing, collapsing, breathless. She stood silent for a moment, before calling them back. Yusuf pulled Abdullahi up from the ground. He giggled and tried to resist, and then gave in.

Ayaan said, "How can I reach you now, if we have a problem?"

I looked at the boys, holding Ayaan's hands again, but tickling each other behind her back. "I'm sorry," I said. "It doesn't make any difference. I'm leaving the office soon."

Ayaan stared at me. She let the boys go and they ran off, chasing each other again.

She said, "But, my sister... who will look after our case?"

I told her one of my colleagues would take over my files, and would help her as best as she could. Ayaan looked crestfallen. "But you're the only one who has known our story from the start."

I assured her I would tell my colleague everything, before she took over the case.

Ayaan turned around to watch the boys then pulled her headscarf tight and turned back.

She said, "The money, the application to the US, you helped us so much. Without that, I would still be working... selling myself, and the children would have no hope for the future at all. At least now, if the US takes us, my children can go to school. They will all work, they'll be teachers and doctors. I won't let any of them be like me."

I looked away, then back to her. "Ayaan, what I did, you know that was only my job. And your children – I'm sure what you say will be true. But they are lucky to have a mother as strong as you."

Ayaan nodded absently and then said, "When are you leaving?"

I told her, "In two weeks. I won't leave without saying goodbye."

She turned to beckon the boys, and I thought of something suddenly. "Ayaan," I said, smiling. "I found a man I like." I was referring to Judah.

Ayaan turned back. She clapped her hands. "I knew it! Every day, I was praying you'd find a husband. Allah is good. He let me thank you this way. Is he a good man?"

I nodded. "And handsome too."

Ayaan cheered and pulled me close to her, embraced me tight. I could see the policeman behind the gate watching us closely now, another standing, leaning forward to see us better. Ayaan, still holding me, almost rocking me, said "I knew he would hear me. Alhamdulillah. Allah is good. My sister, I am so happy. This is all I wanted. Now I can go, start my new life, and feel good that this has come to you." She grasped my hands tightly. "I will thank Allah for hearing my prayers."

She called to the boys and they came running. She tied Abdullahi into a kanga on her back. He waved both his hands in goodbye. Ayaan clutched my arm before leaving and said, again, "Thank you, my sister. And Alhamdulillah"

I walked back toward the office, but when I reached the entrance, turned back to wave once more at Ayaan. But now the police had surrounded her. They were gesturing angrily, and she was shaking her head. Yusuf was tugging frantically on her skirt. One of the policemen shouted, "You know the rules!"

Ayaan nodded slowly at him, then turned to Yusuf, took his hand, and walked away. I wanted to call, to run after her, but a policeman looked up suddenly and I crouched down on the entrance step. I watched as Ayaan disappeared, Yusuf crying now, Abdullahi, distressed, trying to wave down to him, then, defeated, ashamed, lowered my head to my hands.

I didn't see Ayaan in the two weeks before I left the office, and, busy packing up, didn't have time to call her. On my last day at work, I found her number in her file and saved it in my phone.

On the morning I was due to leave Uganda, with half an hour until my taxi for the airport would arrive, I remembered that I still hadn't called her. I looked around. Everything was packed, finally. There was time. I lifted my phone and scrolled down to her number. I called and she answered in Somali. "Ayaan?" I asked. "It's me."

There was silence, then Ayaan spoke. "Hello, my sister." Her voice sounded anxious. "Do you have news on my case?"

"No," I told her, "I'm sorry. Your case has been assigned to my colleague now. She'll call you as soon as there's any update."

"Oh." Ayaan sounded confused.

"I'm just phoning to tell you that I'm leaving now."

"Can I come to the office to see you first?" She asked.

"No," I told her. "I'm at home, about to go for the airport. I'm leaving for good. I just wanted to say goodbye."

"My sister," Ayaan began, panic rising in her voice. "But if you are leaving, what will happen to us?"

"My colleague will look after you," I said. "When the US has made a decision on your case, she will get in touch."

"But only you know my case," Ayaan persisted. She sounded like she was fighting tears. In the background, I could hear girls laughing, and then a baby beginning to cry. Ayaan said something to the children in Somali, then returned to me. The children's noise moved further away.

"Only you have been working with me from the start."

"I know," I said. Then, "Do you have email?" I asked her.

She told me that she did not.

"I just asked because then you could have contacted me when you arrived in the resettlement country."

"Oh," she said. "I don't have it."

I didn't know what else to say, so I wished her luck for the future, for her new life in another country, for the future of her children. I told her, again, that my colleague would follow up on her case.

"Ok," Ayaan said. She didn't sound convinced. She thanked me once more and said goodbye, the tremble in her voice unmistakable now. I didn't hear from her again.

Gone

I checked in at Entebbe airport, made my way to the departure gate, and sat down on a long perforated metal seat. The PA system announced the imminent departure of flights for Nairobi and Bujumbura. I was flying overnight to London Heathrow, and from there to Dublin.

A group of lost-looking African passengers arrived at the gate. They were clutching identical plastic bags with the logo for the International Organization for Migration – IOM – emblazoned on the side. I watched them for a moment, then realized, suddenly, who they must be: a group of the Sudanese refugees we had resettled to Ireland. I knew them from the IOM carrier bags. IOM oversaw this part – the physical relocation – of their resettlement, and the bags served both to identify the refugees to the IOM representative who would meet them at the airport on the other side, and to hold the information leaflets they would need when they arrived. I knew them too from the clothes they were wearing: wrap skirts made from African fabric, donated T-shirts, plastic flip-flops. Hot-weather clothes: they had been living in a settlement in the northernmost reaches of Uganda, the hottest part of the country. They were the only clothes they would have.

The group's resettlement application had been processed months ago, and I didn't know that some of them were due to depart today. There were seventy refugees in all, relocating to a small town in the south of Ireland. The Irish Government was relatively new to resettlement, and had never accepted African refugees before. The decision to take Southern Sudanese refugees was strange: a peace agreement in Southern Sudan had been signed three years earlier in 2005, and many Southern Sudanese refugees were now repatriating to their homeland. They were felt, then, to be less in need of resettlement than other refugees. I wondered why Ireland was not taking Congolese or Somali refugees, who had, at the time, less possibility of returning home safely.

It occurred to me that perhaps there had been some confusion in Ireland, that maybe "Sudanese" refugees were conflated with Darfuri refugees. The war in Darfur – in the west of Sudan – was ongoing and devastating, and many Darfuri refugees were in need of a new home. Southern Sudan, on the other hand, was in 2008 relatively peaceful, and was on course to becoming its own country: it had little to do with Darfur. But perhaps the distinctions mattered little in Ireland. *Sudanese. Southern Sudanese. Darfuri. African.*

I had never before seen refugees I had helped resettle actually depart. My heart quickened: finally, it was real. My work had only ever been abstract: for two years, I had been writing resettlement applications for refugees but had never seen anyone actually leave, and rarely heard from them when they did. I almost didn't believe they really left. But these people – Sudanese refugees who had spent all, or almost all, of their lives in a settlement in northern Uganda – were moving, permanently, to my country, on the same plane as me. For many of them, it would be impossible to afford to return. This would be their last time on African soil. They would become Irish citizens. They would carry a passport with a gold embossed harp on the cover, like mine. Their children would learn to speak Irish, as I had. They would have Irish accents! Some would attend the university I had, live in parts of Dublin where I had lived.

I tried to picture the families in the pebbledash row houses in the small town I knew they were moving to, the sky overcast, the rain always about to fall, the air always damp. I tried to imagine them working in Ireland – cleaning houses, unloading delivery trucks? – I didn't know what work was available to those who spoke no English, and had no literacy or numeracy skills. Few of the Sudanese refugees in the settlements had worked in anything other than subsistence farming. Almost none of the adults could read, write or count. None had running water or electricity. Often, they didn't know how to operate a light switch, a flush toilet. I tried to picture the children in Irish schools, with other kids who had laptops and cell phones.

Would their lives be better? Did reliable access to food and more solid shelter make up for the loss of community, of support, of a culture that was their own? But in Ireland they would have access to education too, and healthcare. Their children would have many more opportunities, for learning and for work, than in a Ugandan settlement. I had seen too many refugees die from diseases that could easily be treated in Europe. In Ireland, their healthcare would be, for the most part, free.

I had spent two years wondering about the business of resettlement, about its worth. Millions of dollars were spent on resettling a tiny minority – in Uganda, fewer than one percent – of refugees to other, wealthier countries. I wondered if it wouldn't be better to spend the money on developing educational opportunities, healthcare, and jobs in Uganda for a much larger number of refugees.

As I sat waiting for the boarding announcement, a young teenage boy in the Sudanese group saw me watching them and smiled. I waved and moved closer to him. I knew from his age that he would likely have grown up in Uganda, and speak good English as a result.

"Are you moving to Ireland?"

He nodded. "I've never been on an airplane. I'm so excited, I won't be able to sleep."

I told him I worked for UNHCR, but was from Ireland, and he nodded politely. He said his name was Francis.

"Are you looking forward to living in Ireland?" I asked him.

He smiled. "I heard that they like football there. I like football. I hope I will be able to play a lot."

I laughed. "It's true. They like football." I thought of the small-town football team in Ireland that was now, I heard, made up in large part of Nigerian immigrants. It was trashing all the other teams in the country. I thought back to seven years earlier, when, traveling alone in Zanzibar, I had gotten lost in Stone Town and required the help of two young boys to walk me back to my hotel. They, too, were eager to make conversation with me about football in Ireland. "Do you know Roy Keane?" they'd asked, as I'd tried to conceal my bemusement.

I thought as well of the many conversations I'd had about football with refugees in the last two years. British soccer was huge in Africa: it was an easy topic of conversation. It was a uniting factor: something I could talk about with people who otherwise had very different backgrounds to mine. It felt surreal to read up on British soccer teams so I could talk more about them with African refugees.

The call to board the plane came over the PA system and the Sudanese group stood, appearing confused. We formed a line. On the plane, I was seated opposite Francis. True to his word, he didn't sleep during the journey. He, and the other children with him, watched from the window, watched the crew, the other passengers. They had no toys, or electronics, or books.

I couldn't sleep either. After two years, I was leaving. I planned to apply for another post, but as yet I didn't know where. I watched Francis and his friends as they pointed out the window. The sky was growing darker. I knew what families like his would have endured in Southern Sudan. War for over twenty years, hunger and disease, then forced displacement to Uganda. The boy was most likely born in Uganda, in a refugee settlement, where living conditions were dire.

For two years, I'd been hearing stories that were similar – and often worse – to what I imagined Francis's family had experienced in Southern Sudan. The horror that refugees had endured before they fled made me feel despair. But sometimes, the horror was too big, too awful, to comprehend or feel. Sometimes, it was too out of reach, too far from my experience, to imagine. Sometimes I chose not to imagine it.

The way that refugees were treated by us, by our organization, was more immediate and impossible to ignore. Our organization was the place, the people, to whom refugees, having fled war, torture and rape, turned for help. When they finally reached the doors of the local NGO where we met them, they appeared exhausted, desperate, but relieved. *At last I'm here: I am safe now.* They made this journey in search of assistance or salvation, only to find, in many cases, that they were rejected or treated with contempt. Often, they said that this rejection was harder to take than the persecution they had endured. *What now?* they said: *Where to turn?*

I was part of the organization, and so felt implicated. I hadn't challenged Godfrey, the senior manager, about his policy of refugees not being able to approach our own office: I was certain that it wouldn't have changed his mind and would have resulted in him punishing me, nothing else. I wasn't able to intervene with the armed police who turned refugees away from our gate: they were carrying out orders. This was the organization, the policies, I was associated with, part of. I felt defeated, ashamed.

The human interactions I had had with refugees – the conversations about soccer, or food, or coffee, about finding me a husband – were a small consolation, a comfort. No matter what happens, I told myself, there are small human joys, and connections in those. We can eat together. We can chat about soccer teams. We can be attracted to each other. Fostering those connections with clients helped me feel that we could transcend the barriers between us, and still find joy; still relish the things that made us human. It helped me believe that, amidst the barbarity, we *were* still human.

Our plane landed in Heathrow, and we – the Sudanese refugees and I – boarded another plane there for Ireland. At arrivals in Dublin, I was met by my father, who helped carry my two cases – everything else had been shipped – to the car. The Sudanese refugees, underdressed for the cold, clutching the plastic bags containing IOM information leaflets in lieu of hand luggage, and in most instances with no checked baggage at all, stood in a group, looking overwhelmed and exhausted. I knew that someone from IOM would come to meet them, and bring them to their new homes – the terraced brick houses with flushing toilets that would replace the mud-brick huts in the settlement that had been their homes until now.

I wanted to see them at least be met at arrivals, but the IOM delegate hadn't arrived when I left. With my father beside me, I maneuvered my luggage cart through the crowds of people in Arrivals – families, nervous men alone clutching flowers, excited children. I looked back. The Sudanese group was still standing there, quiet, some of the women soothing babies, some of the children holding the plastic bags to their chests. They looked cold. Some of the children were shivering. I looked around for the person who would meet them, who would reassure them, and bring them home. I didn't see anyone. Francis spotted me and waved. He appeared exhausted but he was swinging his bag and smiling, like he could not quite rein in his excitement. Not knowing what else to do, I gave him a thumbs-up for good luck. He smiled more now, his expression bemused. I looked at the group once last time, silently wishing, hoping, for them, then turned and made my way through the crowds, so that the next time I looked back, searching for them, they were gone.

VI. SOMEWHERE ELSE

You Changed My Life

After leaving Uganda, I was hired by another agency that deployed resettlement staff to UNHCR offices all over the world. I got married to Judah, whom I had finally flown to meet in the US, after months of talking by phone in Uganda. Our wedding took place under a handmade huppah on a small, picturesque piece of land in New Mexico, where he was from. Since Judah worked from home, he would be able to accompany me on other posts overseas.

Since in many cases it took years for refugees to depart, a lot of my clients had not left Uganda by the time I had. I wondered, always, about their fates.

I thought often of Ayaan, and her praying for me to find a husband. I wished I could tell her that Judah and I were, in fact, now married. And I would smile to myself thinking of her reaction if I told her that Allah had a sense of humor, since the husband he had sent me was a Jew.

I thought about Celestin a lot too. Occasionally, I would wear the blue rooster top he had given me, though not the frilly skirt. Laura emailed me an update while I was posted to Jordan in 2009. She told me that Celestin had left six months after I had, and that before then, had begun identifying openly as a woman, using the new name *Celeste*. She wrote, "Celeste was excited about Canada. She was looking forward to leaving all this behind."

Canada. Life there would surely be easier than in Uganda for a transgender woman. But still, I wondered whether Celeste was lonely. She spoke no English and very little French. Did she have friends there? A partner? What work would she do? Would she be exploited there too?

Laura also updated me on Mario, with whom I had lost touch. He had, she told me, been forced to leave the country. His name had finally appeared in the paper, and he'd lost his job. A man Laura knew, a local gay activist, had been killed.

In the months following our meeting, Sofia, the UNHCR investigator, had contacted me sporadically, requesting emails from Frieda – those in which she had told me of Ali's warning that she would never work for the UN again if she reported what Mamadou had done, and to confirm notes she had taken in the interview. The investigation was drawn out, but I tried to stay patient, hopeful. And then I stopped hearing from her completely. An autoreply to an email told me she was on maternity leave.

In 2009, still in Jordan, I emailed her again, asking for an update, not having heard from her for months. Her reply was curt:

The persons involved are now separated from service.

Separated from service? I emailed her again, to ask what that meant. Two weeks later she replied. *Mamadou and Ali have left, and Linda has retired.*

I sat back, sinking into my chair. That was it? Ali, Mamadou and Linda had received their salaries for over two years after everything had happened; Ali had even received his without working. And who knew what Mamadou had done to other staff during this time. Had there even been an investigation? Had Mamadou and Ali simply resigned? If they had no black mark against their names, they'd quickly be able to find jobs – even other UN posts – again. Linda had retired, as she'd already planned to do. I knew the legend of UN pensions – how generous they were. I knew that she would be living in luxury now, that her decision to protect Mamadou and the reputation of her office, and to lie to us, to choose not to protect others like us – would have had no consequences. No one other than Sofia and perhaps one or two others in an irrelevant, impotent office in Geneva, would have even known what had happened.

I wrote back to Sofia. *Were Mamadou and Ali fired?*

An autoreply this time said that she was no longer working for UNHCR at all.

For years, I had clung to the hope that Sofia – her office – would finally bring justice. I felt like my disillusionment was complete.

A few months after this, I received an email from Lars, the former intern; he now had a temporary post in Uganda. Godfrey was still there, he said, and had recently sent out an email to senior staff. He had sent it in the context of even greater hostility towards gays in Uganda, and a bill proposing the death penalty for "aggravated homosexuality." In his email, Lars told me, Godfrey had written that homosexuality was a "perversion of human sexuality" that was only brought to Africa by the white man. He had ended the statement with a quote from Leviticus.

I wrote back to him. Had anyone challenged him or reported him?

Lars responded that no one had challenged him, even though he had sent the email to the head of office. I sat back and re-read what he had written. The office was mandated – and well-funded – to protect all refugees in Uganda. Gay or transgender refugees, like Celeste, who had been detained and beaten by police at least thirteen times, needed that protection perhaps more than any others. The person charged with providing that, and paid a huge salary to do so, was making clearer than ever that he did not believe these refugees were worthy of protection.

I scrolled through the email address book and found the address of the ethics department of our office in Geneva. I copied and pasted Lars's email into my message, pointing out that this had been sent to senior staff, including the head of office. The following day, I received a reply to say that my report had been received. I received no other emails after that. When I wrote again for an update, I received no response.

✳✳✳

In 2011, based at a UNHCR regional office in Kenya, I had access to a central database of refugees resettled out of east Africa. I realized that now I could find out what had happened to some of my clients from Uganda. In many cases, I could not remember all of the person's names, or the correct spellings, necessary to retrieve the information. But I could remember Ayaan's. I entered all three of her names into the search field. I felt nervous, tapping my foot fast, waiting for the screen to bring up the results. What if she had never left Uganda? What if she was still there, still working as a sex worker, still ostracized by other Somalis because she had an Ethiopian son? What if my colleagues had dropped her case after I left? What if she had died from AIDS?

The screen blinked and the results came up, finally, green lettering on black. She had gone. Two years earlier, a year after I had last seen her, she and her children had left, permanently, for the US.

I sat back, pleased, relieved, but also anxious for her. The US. This was my base now too between postings, since it was Judah's homeplace. I wondered where Ayaan was living, and how her children were doing. Were they at school there? College? Did they have friends?

Months before moving to Kenya, I had lost my daughter in pregnancy. We hadn't named her – it was too painful – and called her only by the nickname we had used for her when I was pregnant. If she had lived, I had thought of giving her – as a middle name, perhaps – Ayaan's name.

Now, living in Nairobi, I was pregnant again. I wanted to contact Ayaan, though I knew I could not. I wanted to tell her about my daughter, and about the baby in my belly, whose image in mysterious, grainy, ultrasound shots I stared at in wonder. My atheism notwithstanding, I wanted to thank her praying for me, to tell her about the babies I had conceived with the man she prayed to come into my life. *These kids came into existence because of you!* I wanted to joke with her. I wanted to tell her, *You changed my life more than I changed yours.*

***

I left Kenya, gave birth to a son, and later had another son too. Judah and I bought a house in New Mexico, with a garden that we loved. The fruit trees had been planted by the previous owners, and gave us more fruit than we could eat. We learned to can or dry it, and went from door to door on our street, giving half of it away.

I unpacked all the boxes I had shipped, finally, and hung the painting that Martha's parents had given me – *Flower Paintings* – the one that had led me to her house, and to everything that followed, over an armchair by the wood stove.

***

In 2014, I decided to look Ali up. It seemed he was now working for a different UN office in the US. His attempt to coerce his intern into not reporting the sexual harassment she had endured, had not in fact prevented him from continuing to work.

I thought about Godfrey. Had he finally been fired? I had reported him again while in Kenya, when I discovered he was still, in spite of the homophobic email and refusal to let refugees approach the office, working in Uganda. Had my reports finally caught up with him? I searched for him online. His photo came up immediately. He was dressed in a shirt and tie, his expression self-satisfied. I read the accompanying article. It stated that he had been promoted several levels – to head of an entire UNHCR regional operation. I was shocked even if, now, it was to be expected. I wondered about the refugees approaching that office for help. Had he instituted a policy there too to ban them from coming onto the premises? Where would gay refugees there be able to turn?

Somewhere Else

While living in the US between deployments, I decided to volunteer with a local organization that assisted refugees who had just been resettled to the country. The organization told me that the refugees in the area were from Burundi, Rwanda, Somalia, Ethiopia, Nepal, Cuba and Iraq. I was looking forward to seeing, finally, how their lives after resettlement were.

Judah and I signed up to help recently-resettled teenage refugees with homework. Staff at the organization picked the teenagers up from school twice a week and brought them to the office, where they could work with adult volunteers who would help them with whatever they needed: English, math, physics, biology, college applications. The teenagers were mostly Iraqi, Burundian and Nepalese; the volunteers were mainly retirees, including more than one PhD physicist from the national laboratories based nearby. Judah, an engineer, was assigned to work with students who needed help with science and math; my skill set was a little less clear, and I was matched with students who brought college and scholarship forms to fill out.

When we began volunteering, some of the Iraqi students had just arrived in the country. They were struggling with the new school system, with the culture, and more than anything, with having to learn and communicate entirely in a new language. They were isolated and depressed. Slowly over time, we saw that they gained in confidence and spoke of enjoying school now and making friends. Eventually, they spoke excellent English too.

Other students adapted more quickly. A fifteen-year-old Burundian girl who had been in the country for only three years and hadn't spoken English before arriving, was already captain of her school's cheerleading team and top of her class in math. A 16-year-old Sudanese boy travelled throughout the US, representing the state in track and field.

One afternoon, I was assigned to work with Claude, a Rwandan teenager. Claude had never actually been to Rwanda. His mother had fled the genocide in 1994 while pregnant with him, and given birth to him in a refugee camp in Tanzania. Claude had lived in the camp until he was fifteen. His father had disappeared during the genocide and never been found. It was assumed that he had been murdered. In 2009, after fifteen years of living in a camp, Claude, his mother, three older siblings, and grandmother were resettled to the US.

Claude was friends with another teenager who had fled from Burundi to a different camp in Tanzania, and from there been resettled to the US. They did not attend the same school, so only met up at the after-school group. They high-fived and greeted each other in Swahili, laughing, when they met up.

Claude had requested assistance with both his college and scholarship applications. He was applying to study Nursing at the local university. When we sat down together, he pulled out a file, in which the forms had been neatly categorized in clear plastic sleeves. He passed me one of the papers. It was a letter of reference from one of his teachers. She had written of his extraordinary level of commitment to his work, and his determination in the face of challenges – a new language, new culture – when he had first arrived. She talked about how friendly and helpful he was in class, and what a wonderful nurse he would make.

I skimmed the photocopy of the application form. The first question after the section for basic information asked for reasons for applying. "Why do *you* think you'd make a good nurse?" I asked Claude.

His expression was serious. "Because I'm good-looking."

I laughed, and the girls sitting at the table beside ours, giggled, nudging each other, and Claude laughed too.

We worked on a draft of the form together, then turned to the application for financial help. The first question asked why he needed this help. He said, "My sisters and brother were already over eighteen when they arrived in the US, so they didn't go to high school here. It's hard for them to find work as they don't speak good English. I need a scholarship so I can support my family."

I stopped writing and looked at him. The scholarship amount would barely support one person, let alone six.

"What is your living situation?" I asked him, turning to the next question.

He answered, "The six of us live in a two-bedroom apartment. My mother, grandmother and sister share one bedroom, and my brothers and I share another. The apartment is very small."

I knew from his address that he lived in a rough part of town. All of the newly-resettled refugees were accommodated in tiny apartments in large complexes in sketchy parts of the city. Very few could afford to move out.

Claude talked of his excitement at the possibility of attending university, and of eventually becoming a nurse. "When I lived in the camp, this was my dream, but I never thought it would be possible. I didn't think I would even have the chance to finish high school."

I thought about Claude living in the camp for fifteen years, knowing the living conditions there: the small mud-brick huts and shared latrines; the crowded, basic shack-classrooms and medical facilities. I thought about his journey to get here: the endless interviews and interrogations and years of waiting. His arrival here: the culture shock and having to negotiate everything, including school, in an alien language. The poverty and isolation and loneliness his family must be experiencing now. His optimism and cheerfulness bewildered and lifted me. A former colleague had told me once, *Resettlement is for the children. We lose the adults. But sometimes the children do thrive. And* their *children even more.*

Some would thrive. And many that I met while volunteering, did. I still wasn't sure that the money spent on resettling a tiny percentage of refugees couldn't be better spent on helping to create job opportunities and improving the conditions of *all* of those who fled. But Claude's optimism gave me some cheer. Perhaps some of the refugees I had worked with were doing well now, in spite of what they'd fled from, and how they'd been treated by some of the people charged with helping them: the whole huge mess.

***

When my children were one and a half and almost-three, I brought them with me on deployment to Senegal for a year. It was the first posting I'd taken since they were born. My older son had a head full of solutions: *let's go to the hardware store and buy tools to make new homes for refugees! What about these empty houses? Why can't the people you work with live there?* He made up a game that he played with the oscillating floor-fan in his bedroom. Wherever the fan pointed was where people were being resettled. He asked to send Christmas presents to a camp I worked in in Guinea, toys for the children, but insisted they should be wrapped.

***

The year we returned from Senegal was the year Donald Trump was elected president of the US. Soon after his inauguration, he announced a temporary ban on resettlement of all refugees, and an indefinite ban on Syrian refugees.

My colleagues sent me photos of meetings held to inform refugees that, after years of waiting and having their hopes raised, they would now not be going anywhere. The photos showed rows and rows of people, faces in hands, looking broken. My boss from Senegal told me of Darfuri refugees in Chad – refugees whose cases I had worked on – who had sold their shelters and all of their belongings and travelled for days to reach the airport, only to be told that they could no longer go. This after living in camps for twelve, fourteen years. Now, having sold everything, they didn't even have a home in the camp to go back to.

Our weekends in the US were full of protests and rallies. I joined a march to the airport with my children, now three and four. We and the other protestors sat on the floor in arrivals while security officers, grim-faced and heavily armed, watched us closely. I thought about the thousands of people that I had worked with by this time, of what they had gone through, of the exhaustive security checks they were subjected to before being accepted to the US, of their lives before war, and kidnapping, and torture. I thought of Sadia, the suicidal Somali teenager, and Celeste, the transgender woman who had been arrested and beaten thirteen times, and Ayaan, the woman who was forced to work as a sex-worker and contracted HIV, and the Iraqi man I'd worked with in Jordan in 2009, who had been tortured and shot, and whose friend had been beheaded, and the Darfuri children I'd worked with in the Central African Republic in 2010, whose entire village had been bombed to the ground. I shouted, angry, like the hundreds of other protesters sitting on the filthy airport floor beside me, in front of the row of heavily-armed security, protesting a law that would stop all of these people from being able to find a new home, from being able to start a new life, somewhere else.

I was filled with fury, and despair. So many people supported the ban; so many people agreed – in spite of statistics proving otherwise – that refugees were a security threat, and should be kept out. So many people resisted the facts about what refugees had gone through, and the security checks to which they were subjected. In Europe, people were drowning trying to reach safety, and still, many said they were parasites, unwelcome, that they should stay at home. The hostility felt surreal. How could people feel this way? How could they lack the imagination to understand what people had gone through? How could they not want to let them in? This was where we had ended up?

Other people were outraged, but finally moved on. Court orders put part of the ban on hold, and many people assumed that was it – that refugees were being resettled to the US again. They weren't. Months passed, and processing of resettled refugees still hadn't been resumed. Though it had received less media attention, Trump had also cut the quota for refugees who could be resettled to the US, meaning that no matter what, fewer refugees would be accepted annually than any time since at least 1980.

Regardless of the ban and whether it would be overturned, refugees were screwed.

Since the ban, I had been going after the more hateful and uninformed anti-refugee posts I saw online – responding with facts about resettlement and security checks, and statistics about the numbers of refugees involved in terrorism. I was persistent. I began to feel like I was trolling these people – these commentators spreading hate and misinformation. It made no difference that I could see. People wanted a target for their hatred, their resentment. But I did it anyway. I couldn't think of anything else to do. I wanted to tell people: This is why they fled. You would too. I felt – naively or not – that if they could hear the stories, their hearts would open: that their hatred had only come about because they didn't know.

On 5th September 2017, Donald Trump announced that he was ending DACA – the Deferred Action for Childhood Arrivals immigration policy – in the US. The policy had allowed some of those who had entered the US illegally as children to receive a renewable period of deferred action from deportation, and a work permit. The futures of the 800,000 or so people who relied on this policy were in jeopardy.

On the same day as this announcement, I had my interview to become a citizen of the US. I sat in the waiting room of US Citizenship and Immigration Services, clutching the folders of documents that would prove I was who said I was, that I should be granted this, that I hadn't done anything wrong. Other than lawyers and Judah, I was the only white person in the room: most of the others awaiting interview were Latino, and one couple was African. Walking into the interview room alone, so nervous I could barely speak, I thought: this is how it is to be on the other side. The man across the desk from me held all the power. I had spent hours getting ready, trying to look respectable and responsible, and weeks studying and preparing papers. I had to answer everything right. I was nauseous from worry. Did the man across from me know this? Did he care? Would he be kind? Had I given enough thought – when I had this power – to how the other person on the other side must feel? Was I kind?

But I was wrong: this wasn't how it was for a refugee to be on the other side. My life didn't depend on passing this interview. If I failed, I would get another chance. If I failed again, I could still remain in the US, as a permanent resident. Even if that weren't true, I had British and Irish passports, and could live anywhere in Western Europe. And the odds of not failing were in my favor: English was my first language; it was easy for me to learn what was necessary and fill out the applications. It was easy to say the right thing. And, then, failing all that, I knew that I would be treated with less suspicion. I was white.

My interview lasted fifteen minutes, after which I was told I had passed, and presented with a letter congratulating me on becoming a US citizen. Judah drove me home, then left again to pick our older son up from school.

I turned on the TV. The news was reporting the overturning of DACA. A woman was being interviewed. She had been brought by her parents to the US from Mexico as a toddler, and never returned. She didn't speak Spanish. She had no memories of Mexico; the US was the only home she knew. She was studying for her third university degree. Now, with this new ruling, she was in danger of being deported – to a place where she had no family she knew, no connections at all, and where she didn't speak the language. I looked at the letter in my hands.

You passed the tests of English and U.S. history and government. Congratulations! Your application is recommended for approval. At this time, it appears that you have established your eligibility for naturalization.

My journey was easy. I had filled out forms, had two brief interviews – one for my Green Card and one for my citizenship – and I would attend a swearing-in ceremony. That was it. It was delusional to think I knew, even eleven years after I had begun working with refugees, and after going through these immigration hurdles, how refugees felt.

***

By 2019, there were over 70 million forcibly displaced people worldwide. Against this backdrop, in September 2019, Trump declared his intention to end refugee resettlement completely. Soon after, his administration announced it would set a cap of 18,000 refugees for the fiscal year, and allow states to ban resettlement outright. While the figure of 18,000 would be an all-time low – in Obama's last year in office, for example, the cap had been 110,000 – even that didn't reflect the reality. The administration had carved up the quota into categories of people it desired. 5,000 of the spots would be reserved only for people fleeing religious persecution – under Trump, a much higher percentage of Christians was being resettled than ever before. 4,000 slots would be for Iraqis who helped the US. 1,500 would be for people from El Salvador, Honduras and Guatemala – presumably to deter those people from showing up at the border to seek asylum themselves.

Only 7,500 spots would be left for everyone else: those like the people I worked with in Uganda, along with millions of refugees elsewhere, would have to be squeezed into this allowance. In addition, over 100 resettlement offices in the US were closed, meaning less help for those who did reach the country. Family reunification, overseen by those offices, would now be much more difficult.

Trump's changes would be tantamount to destroying the resettlement program altogether, at a time when there were more refugees than ever before. The Guardian quoted the director of policy and advocacy at Church World Services as saying, "This is actually the United States becoming a bad actor when it comes to refugee protection. This is the United States saying – during a time when the world is facing the largest displacement crisis in history – the US is going to roll up its mat and go home."

I recalled Sadia's words often: life is too much suffering. I had no answers to anything. My own motives for doing the work I did were flawed and messy. I wanted to do something useful, but I also wanted to escape from the person that I was – afraid that I would succumb to depression as Martha had. I wanted to feel worthwhile. Sometimes I wondered if the thing I wanted to do most was just hear the stories, so I could try to pass them on.

I had friends who had turned to this work for similar reasons to mine. Others wanted UN jobs for the money. Some, and this was worse, for the power.

I wondered if the work I did was good, or good enough. Often, following the announcement of the refugee resettlement ban, I would feel dismayed, ready to give up, and then feel furious, and want to fight again.

Sometimes, in the US between deployments, I would occasionally sift through the boxes I had shipped from the countries I had lived and worked in. Once, years after leaving Uganda, I would find the note Celeste had written for me, on graph paper, years before:

My life has changed since I met you, you have saved me from sorrows and worries.

I read it over and over, trying to believe it, until the paper tore at the folds.

Acknowledgments

Versions of the chapters "What It's Like" and "Every Drop Counts" were previously published in *The Dublin Review*.

Thank you to Mesa Refuge and Blue Mountain Center for giving me the gifts of time and beautiful surroundings that made it possible to complete this book.

For feedback and support, thank you to Dirt City Writers, the writers of Ellen's apartment, Greg Martin, Nell McShane Wulfhart, Brendan Barrington, Sibyl Ruth and Aki Schilz at The Literary Consultancy, and Zoe Ross at United Agents.

Thank you to Natasha Ward and Marsha Shandur for giving me, a stranger, a free home, so I could undertake the Human Rights MA that led to all the work that followed. I have been trying to repay that karma since.

And to everyone in this book who shared their story with me, thank you, and as you have told me, in French, *Courage*.

Word-of-mouth is crucial for any author to succeed. If you enjoyed the book, please leave a review online—anywhere you are able. Even if it's just a sentence or two. It would make all the difference and would be very much appreciated.

About the Author

Karen O'Reilly is from Northern Ireland. She has worked for the UN refugee agency in Uganda, Jordan, the Central African Republic, Kenya, Senegal and Guinea. She has interviewed and reviewed the cases of several thousand refugees from all over Africa and the Middle East, including Sierra Leonean child soldiers, Congolese human rights activists, Iraqi dissidents, Ethiopian military pilots, and Rwandan genocide survivors. She has served as an expert witness in close to one hundred asylum cases in the UK and US.

Thank you so much for reading one of our **Biography / Memoirs**.

If you enjoyed our book, please check out our recommended title for your next great read!

Z.O.S. by Kay Merkel Boruff

"...dazzling in its specificity and intensity."

–C.W. Smith, author of *Understanding Women*

Made in the USA
Middletown, DE
29 September 2020